Get Published!

Get Published!

Professionally, Affordably, Fast

SUSAN DRISCOLL

AND

DIANE GEDYMIN

iUniverse, Inc.
New York Lincoln Shanghai

Get Published!
Professionally, Affordably, Fast

For the most up-to-date information on iUniverse prices and policies, please call or visit our Web site; iUniverse books may be ordered through booksellers or by contacting:

iUniverse
2021 Pine Lake Road, Suite 100
Lincoln, NE 68512
www.iUniverse.com
1-800-Authors (1-800-288-4677)

ISBN-13: 978-0-595-39573-6 (pbk)
ISBN-13: 978-0-595-83975-9 (ebk)
ISBN-10: 0-595-39573-2 (pbk)
ISBN-10: 0-595-83975-4 (ebk)

Printed in the United States of America

Five copies of the book and cover of *Get Published!* were printed in just one minute using print-on-demand digital technology. Printed in the United States by Lightning Source Inc.

CONTENTS

Part 2: Get Informed

Part 3: Get Support

ACKNOWLEDGMENTS

Our special thanks to Lynn Everett who worked tirelessly as editor of this book while continuing to do her job as managing editor of iUniverse; we really couldn't have finished this book without her professional guidance and straightforward reality checks!

And deep appreciation to Randy Bright for his commitment to creating the book's artwork in a way that helps readers visualize complicated ideas at a glance, and for designing the book's cover at the eleventh hour.

Others at iUniverse worked to get this book done professionally and fast—our thanks to Holly Beermann, Joyce Greenfield, Rachel Krupicka, and Sarah Wischhof for reading the manuscript to make sure that what we say is what we do; to Joyce Greenfield for carefully overseeing the production; and to Pam Anderson for making sure the book is printed and distributed on time. And to members of the editorial department—Sally Peterson, Sarie Whitson, and Lynn Holm—our gratitude for keeping things going while Lynn devoted so much of her time to editing this book. In our Shanghai office, thanks to Jane Cao for the interior design, to Hattie Yang for carefully checking for errors, and to Lisa Chen for coordinating such a fast turnaround.

Thanks to Kim Hawley, Steve Riggio, and Marcella Smith for their "outside" reads to make sure we clearly explained our ideas and programs to the public; and to Patricia Bostelman, Roger Chiocci, and Meg Hogan for their help with the merchandising of the book. Thanks to Brian Jud for his advice on the marketing chapters.

And last, but not least, to Molly Redenbaugh who helped us to get this project going at the start, and who cracked the whip along the way!

Thanks to all.

YOU CAN BE
A PUBLISHED AUTHOR

Many people think that publishing a book is an enterprise for an elite few. Although that may have been true in bygone days, now publishing is easier, faster, and more affordable than ever.

Advances in technology and distribution have given birth to a relatively new model of publishing that enables you to see and hold your professionally published book in record time, allows readers to purchase your book online or through retail stores, and, perhaps most importantly, gives you a chance to pursue commercial success and create a lasting legacy.

The technology that makes all of this possible is called print-on-demand (POD), which allows professional-quality books to be affordably printed for virtually anyone in quantities as little as one copy at a time. In fact, the book you're now reading was printed using POD technology.

One of the most established and respected providers of POD technology is a nontraditional book publisher called iUniverse. At iUniverse, however, we go beyond offering innovative methods of printing and distributing books; the services we offer, which include editorial and marketing services in addition to printing and distribution, rival the range and quality of those you'd expect from a mainstream publisher.

Having said that, our main goal at iUniverse is to help aspiring authors achieve their dreams of getting published, and we recognize that authors now have many viable alternatives to make that happen. If you are a hardworking writer who dreams of seeing your book in print, we think

---

Print-on-Demand—A Revolution in Publishing

According to author Tracy Mayor in the May 15, 2004, edition of the online newsletter *CIO: The Resource for Information Executives*, print-on-demand publishing is "steadily upending the way people make books." Although POD publishing is still considered only "a small piece of the printing market…it's the chunk with the largest growth potential." The retail value of POD, she writes, is expected to jump from $33.2 billion in 2003 to $60.2 billion by 2008, a 13 percent increase compounded annually.

---

you deserve to have a positive publishing experience, regardless of whether you choose to sign with a traditional house, choose to self-publish completely on your own, or seek help through supported self-publishing through iUniverse. We want to give you all the information you need to make sure that dream doesn't end up a nightmare.

This book will guide you through the entire publishing process, from writing your first draft all the way through marketing and selling your published book. You'll learn about the different models of publishing, hear from published authors, and—we hope, ultimately—be inspired to write your own book and *Get Published!*

Part 1

GET STARTED

Chapter 1

WHY WRITE?

All writers at one time or another—even those whose names you know and whose work has been studied in countless classrooms and book groups over the years—have asked themselves, "Why write?"

The initial answer to this question is unique to each writer. For some, the very act of writing is satisfying and therapeutic, as it is for poets who write purely for the joy of it as inspiration strikes and for diarists who journal their most intimate thoughts for no one's eyes but their own.

Ultimately, though, many writers yearn to be read by others and to gain recognition, and money, for their hard work. If you don't believe it, get a group of serious writers together and listen to what they have to say. They may start by discussing technique and execution, such as how to maintain the point of view, develop a plot, or use a semicolon. Before long, however, the conversation inevitably shifts. Someone drops a tidbit such as "I queried three agents last week," and the others immediately want to know who the agents were and how the writer went about making his query. Eventually, everyone in the room begins dreaming and can't wait to get their words into print.

So why do *you* write? The fact that you're reading this book says a lot about your answer. It's a pretty good bet that you write because you have something to say, something you want others to read. But to be read, your book must be published.

A Solitary Art...Sort Of

The act of writing, by its very nature, is a solitary one. But for the product of your time and effort to have broader meaning, it must be shared.

In addition, there's something validating about being able to point to a printed piece with your name on the cover. It marks you as a professional writer to family members, friends, and even those casual acquaintances you may meet at a party who want to know what you do. Lots of people say they want to write, but if you have a published book, you hold the proof that you not only can write but also actually have written. Handing someone a copy of your book is saying, "I'm a writer—a published one!"

Everybody Has a Story to Tell

"I can't help thinking there's a book in this."

Have you ever finished reading a book and said to yourself, "I could have written that!" We all have experiences, stories, and ideas that others likely want to read about. Whether it's a how-to manual for an unusual hobby, a cookbook of favorite family recipes, a memoir about growing up in a foreign country, or a novel based on recollections of an earlier era, we all have the makings of a book inside us.

Just because everyone has a story waiting to come out, however, doesn't mean it always will. Millions of people—83 percent of Americans, in fact—say they want to write a book. Yet few ever do.

As any published writer will tell you, in addition to talent, you must possess equal amounts of persistence and determination. It's one thing to carry around a story in your head; it's quite another to be able to sit in front of a computer until you get it all down in writing. Are you up to the challenge? If your answer is yes, then by all means, go for it. But do some planning first—a little preparation now will pay off down the line.

ASKING THE BIG QUESTION

Too many manuscripts never get beyond the first chapter, and those that do generally bog down somewhere in the middle because their authors started writing too soon. They jumped straight into the writing without taking time to prepare. Remember, you're not in a race against time to see how fast you can publish a book. Your objective is to write the best book you can, no matter how much or how little effort and time it may take.

Embarking on a long road trip without a planned destination will get you nowhere fast. In the same way, beginning your book without an idea of where you want it to end up will inevitably bring you to a dead end. Before you put your fingers to the keyboard, you need to get a pretty good idea of where you're going and who your audience is.

Ask yourself the following question: why am I writing this book? Is it...

- **For family and friends?** Personal or family histories can be a good way to tell your life story to a small circle of interested readers and to leave behind a legacy for your future generations to enjoy.

- **For catharsis?** Writers sometimes pen their memoirs as a way to bring up issues they need to confront to move on with their lives.

- **Because you're an expert on the subject?** Self-help books are the perfect vehicle for imparting your knowledge about a subject to colleagues on a professional level or in a way that is appealing and accessible to the general public.

- **For professional recognition?** If you have advice about a particular business activity or success secrets to share, writing a book may well be the way to do that, as well as an avenue for enhancing your reputation and improving your professional standing within your industry.

- **To back up a presentation you're giving?** Motivational speakers often write self-help books that are especially suited for "back-of-the-room" sales—that is, sales made directly to attendees at the seminar or conference. Offering a book to take home after a presentation lends authenticity and credibility to the message.

- **To launch a writing career?** Is there a novel inside of you fairly bursting to come out? Characters that won't let you rest? A story you just *have* to tell? People who have a passion for writing are willing to devote the time and energy it takes to complete a manuscript as a way of finding their voice and honing their craft.

FINDING THE RIGHT ANSWER

Now that you've devoted a lot of time and serious thought to your book's purpose and prospective readers, it's time to make some decisions.

Determining your book's purpose and potential audience in advance will help you decide how much time, money, and effort you want to devote to your writing. For example, if you simply want to document your family's history to share it with relatives at the next big reunion, you probably don't need to worry about doing extensive research on various historical periods or incorporating universal themes—unless, of course, yours is a special situation. Say you're helping your grandfather write a World War II memoir and he's a retired history professor. In that case, it might be a good idea to hire a professional researcher to verify the names and dates your grandfather recalls to preserve the professional reputation he's worked so many years to build.

Suppose, instead, that the book you want to write is a contemporary novel set in a place you know firsthand. You may not have to spend much time doing research, but you will need to pay attention to the elements that go into every good piece of fiction—dialogue, characterization, pacing, plot, point of view, and setting.

Or say you're a motivational speaker who sells books to people who attend your seminars—you'll want to be sure to give them their money's worth by incorporating valuable tips they can't get elsewhere as well as all the features of a professionally published work.

In addition to guiding your research and writing efforts, your answers to the questions we've posed will help you work more effectively toward defining, and eventually achieving, your goals.

SETTING ACHIEVABLE GOALS

Tell someone you're a writer, and the questions fly: "How do you work?" "Where do you get your ideas?" "Are you published?"

Then, before you have a chance to answer even the first question, your inquirer deals the definitive *coup de grâce*: "You know, I've always wanted to be a writer myself."

Many people, including perhaps some of your own friends and relatives, entertain the fantasy of becoming a writer. And no wonder: there's a kind of mystique that seems to follow writers. We've come to picture them as tortured souls huddled in darkened garrets, driven to write for the sake of their art.

However, many writers are also driven to write as a money-making career. If you are one of these writers, think of a book as you would any other business project. You wouldn't try to launch a new product without setting goals or land a new client without carefully preparing a presentation. Likewise, you shouldn't try to write a book without some serious planning. If you neglect to think ahead, the odds are better than average that you won't finish the job.

So much has been written on the importance of having and setting goals that the whole idea may seem a little hackneyed and perhaps even overwhelming. Don't be intimidated by the volume of information that's available. Getting your act together is really not all that difficult when you think of the goal-setting process in terms of a simple, memorable acronym: **SMART**.[1]

To be effective, your goals must be:

- **Specific.** This is no time to be vague or ambiguous about what you want. State your goal in specific terms, using numbers whenever possible. Too many people say, "My goal is to write a book." Be more precise. Instead, say, "My goal is to write a 250-page manuscript for a book about winning at tennis (or whatever subject you have in mind)." See the difference? Now you have a specific destination and

---

1   Adapted from Paul J. Meyer's "Attitude is Everything" http://www.topachievement.com/smart.html.

a basic road map on which to chart the steps you'll need to take to get to where you want to be.

- **Manageable.** Be careful not to set goals that you are incapable of achieving or over which you have no control. If you know you are approaching a busy period at work or in your personal life, don't add to your stress by setting an unrealistic deadline for completing your book. Writing a book requires a good deal of time putting pencil to paper or working in front of your computer. Are you prepared to make that kind of commitment? How will you juggle the other priorities in your life? Set your goals accordingly.

- **Attainable.** There's nothing wrong with reaching for the stars, but be careful about setting your goals so high that they are virtually unattainable. The first time you aren't able to meet a goal for whatever reason, you'll be disappointed and discouraged. If it happens often enough, you may give up on your book altogether. Instead of setting big-picture goals that take a long time to achieve, try breaking them up into subgoals that you can attain more readily. For example, instead of saying, "I will complete one chapter per week," make your goal "I will write for two hours a day, five days each week." In all likelihood, the desired outcome (one completed chapter per week) will be the same, but breaking up a weekly goal into daily increments makes it less intimidating and increases your chances of achieving it. The more goals you can achieve, the more likely you'll stick with your project to its completion.

- **Realistic.** When you first get the urge to write a book, everything about your project looks rosy, and you can't wait to get started. But rest assured that as you become more involved, obstacles will happen: the library book that has the information you need to write Chapter 2 will be checked out the week you need it, or the electrical power will go out the very night you planned to put the finishing touches on your introduction. Roadblocks like these are bound to pop up, but when they do, you'll be less likely to quit if you have set realistic, flexible goals.

- **Tied to time.** In his book, *Getting Things Done*, Ed Bliss writes, "The first step in achieving your goals is to recognize that 'someday' is not a day of the week." How many times have you said to yourself, "Someday, I'll make a trip to…" but never actually gotten there? If instead you say, "Next June, I will take a trip to…" you'll probably be shopping for airfares. One of the biggest mistakes goal-setters make is neglecting the element of time. If you want to achieve your goals, set a specific deadline for every one of them and then be accountable for those deadlines as much as it is in your control. It's a lot harder to let a goal slide when you have assigned a date to it. Goals without deadlines are just dreams.

In addition to SMART, remember one more letter when setting your goals. That letter is W, for **Write it down**. As simple as it may sound, you are more likely to achieve your goals if you write them down than if you just leave them floating around in your head. There's something about being able to actually hold a goal in your hand that implies a commitment to it. Statistics show that you are less apt to ignore a goal you can read on paper.

Create a worksheet to set your own personal publishing goals or use the sample we've provided. Keeping SMART in mind, state your goal at the top of the page, then list the steps you will take to achieve it. Be as specific as you can, and don't forget to set those all-important deadlines!

SMART
Goal Worksheet
Create a separate worksheet for each goal

Make every goal **SMART**:
S – Specific
M – Manageable
A – Attainable
R – Realistic
T – Tied to time

Goal:

_____

_____

Action steps: **Due date:**

1. _____ _____

2. _____ _____

3. _____ _____

4. _____ _____

5. _____ _____

6. _____ _____

7. _____ _____

8. _____ _____

9. _____ _____

10. _____ _____

Note: You can download a copy of this, and all the worksheets in this book, from iUniverse.com/getpublished.

A FINAL WORD

One reason that so many more people intend to write a book than actually complete one is that it is easy to become mired in the details. Well-intentioned authors can read every book about writing they come across; attend every writing conference, class, and seminar they can; and obsess over whether their writing is good enough. Be careful that you don't become so invested in the process itself that you never get around to actually writing.

Setting realistic goals can help. It's true that the goals you write down are the goals you're most likely to achieve; the fact that you've committed them to paper, however, doesn't mean they can't be changed. Your goals are on your computer's hard drive, not cast in stone. You can manipulate and adjust them whenever you need to; you can even altogether eliminate those that aren't working.

If you make your writing a chore, it will show. Lighten up and have some fun along your journey from "Chapter 1" to "The End."

WHAT AUTHORS HAVE TO SAY

I was in academia for thirty years, and I wrote six nonfiction books published by mainstream publishers, including two by Columbia University. When I retired at seventy, I returned to school and got an MA from Temple University in creative writing. My dream had always been to write a novel, and now at seventy-four, with the help of iUniverse, I have one published. I chose the print-on-demand route this time because I wanted to be alive when it appeared, and also because I frankly wanted more control over the content than would have been the case with mainstream publishers. My books arrived yesterday afternoon and I'm ecstatic—they look great!

—Hugh Rosen
  Author, *Silent Battlefields*

I've enjoyed a successful broadcasting career for quite some time and had the good fortune to work at a number of very successful radio stations during my career, including WCBS in New York, WBZ in Boston, and KDKA in Pittsburgh. I've always loved to write. And writing and publishing are in the family; my brother-in-law and sister are in the publishing business. After I wrote my novel, my brother-in-law suggested that I contact iUniverse, because "there was a lot of good talk in the industry" about the things they were doing. I researched the company, and…the rest is history. I don't know where my life is taking me, but I'd love to segue into a full-time writing career. I have no delusions of grandeur. I know how difficult it is to succeed in the business, but I have to tell you, part of the fun is trying.

—Jim Harrington
  Author, *Squeeze Play*

My brother George and I grew up on a dairy farm in Rhode Island, the former hunting grounds of the Narragansett Indians. Some of our earliest memories are of going out into the newly plowed fields with our father to look for arrowheads. Both of us came away with a deep respect for the land and for the Native Americans who had gone before us. While working as a special-education teacher, I developed the idea to write a book about the Narragansett Indians. Writing *Cherokee Tears* took me four years, and then George illustrated it. After my agent was unable to place the book with a traditional publisher, I turned to iUniverse. It was the best decision I ever made. George and I don't think *Cherokee Tears* will ever make us rich, but I guess that depends on how you define rich.

—Ann Emmons Petri
  Special-education teacher and author of *Cherokee Tears*

I've been a screenwriter, a journalist, a food-writer, and a published novelist, but when I wrote *Cookin' for Love*, I couldn't find anyone willing to publish it. Traditional publishers told me that no one wanted to read "chick lit" with a middle-aged heroine. That's when I decided to take matters into my own hands and went with iUniverse to help me self-publish my book. It was amazing that, in a matter of mere weeks, the book that no one in the publishing world wanted was selling and selling and selling! In fact, after a mere two weeks on the market, *Cookin' for Love* rose to number twenty-three on Barnes & Noble.com (www.bn.com)—out of more than a million titles. iUniverse gave me something most publishers don't or won't: the opportunity for my book to find its market.

—Sharon Boorstin
 Journalist and author of *Cookin' for Love: A Novel with Recipes*

Chapter 2

FROM DREAM TO COMPLETED MANUSCRIPT

Simply wishing you could write a book won't make it so.

If you are one of the many who aspire to be a published author, we hope you took the advice in the first chapter and gave serious thought to your reasons for writing, as well as your intended audience. If you took the additional step of completing the Goal Worksheet, you will have not only a pretty good idea of where you want to go on your writing journey but also a road map for getting there.

The next step is to put your plan into action. Start by setting aside a place to write and acquiring the necessary tools. Then establish a writing schedule—on paper—and hold yourself to it. In no time at all, your book will begin to take shape.

Tools of the Trade

Every job requires some kind of equipment, and writing is no exception. Here are a few of the tools and supplies you'll want to have on hand as you write your book.

Computer Hardware and Software

Pity poor Shakespeare; he had to create his masterpieces by candlelight with nothing but a quill and ink! You have countless more options available to you. Number one on your must-have list should be a computer. If you don't already have one, or if you need to update the equipment and software you have, here are some things to consider:

- **Laptop or desktop?** The answer to this question largely depends on your budget and how portable you want to be. If you like the idea of being able to take your work wherever you go, whether it's the next room, the local café, or halfway around the world, then a laptop is likely the right choice. Keep in mind, however, that you will have to pay for the privilege of portability, as laptops can sometimes cost twice as much as their desktop counterparts.

- **High-speed Internet.** The Internet is a godsend for writers. Instead of trekking to the library every time you need to do research, you can search for the information you need from the comfort of your own home. Surfing the Web or uploading and downloading files will be far quicker and easier with a high-speed Internet connection, so shop around and go for the fastest service you can afford.

- **Word-processing software.** Writing and revising your manuscript will be considerably easier if you have word-processing software that is especially suited to the task. Although there are several word-processing packages available, Microsoft Word (alone or as part of the Microsoft Office suite) remains the publishing industry standard at the time of this publication. Since its inception in the early 1980s, Word has undergone many improvements that make it writer- and editor-friendly. To take full advantage of any software's capabilities, make sure you are using the newest version on the market. You might also consider investing in a course that will teach you how to use the software to its full potential to help you write and revise your manuscript. Anything that makes it easier to record your thoughts is worth the investment.

- **Printers.** Though you'll likely do all of your writing and most of your revising on-screen and submit your finished book to a publisher electronically, you may still want to print a hard copy of your manuscript from time to time. In fact, many writers like to print their work at the end of every writing day to give themselves a visual reminder of their progress; watching the pages pile up engenders a sense of satisfaction and accomplishment. The kind of printer you buy should depend, again, on your budget and your needs. If you're using your printer solely to turn out manuscript pages for your own use and don't plan to print color photos, there's no need to go too high-tech or to pay extra for color capabilities. An inexpensive monochrome laser or inkjet printer should serve your purpose.

- **Storage.** Last but certainly not least, proper, safe storage of your work is essential. There's nothing more frustrating than losing hours' worth of material in a split second. To prevent this, back up your work electronically, not only when you're finished for the day, but also periodically throughout the writing process—ideally, every twenty to thirty minutes. Moreover, storage *outside* your hard drive is essential. A harsh reality of technology is that computers crash—all the time. Copying files to a CD or using a relatively inexpensive and easy-to-use external storage device provides insurance against losing your work, your time—and maybe even your sanity.

An Inviting Place to Write

As a writer, you can practice your craft anywhere, anytime. Writing doesn't require a lot of expensive or highly sensitive equipment or even a special workspace. All you need is paper and pencil or a laptop, which you can tuck into a briefcase or backpack and carry to the library, the park, or even the beach.

Some writers find they work better away from home. J. K. Rowling is a good example; she wrote her first Harry Potter book at a neighborhood teashop while her baby slept in a stroller nearby.

Regardless of how portable you like to be, it's nice to have a comfortable writing space awaiting your return home. You'll be more apt to want to sit down and get to work if you have an inviting space in which to write and a quiet, out-of-the-way area to keep you focused.

Ideally, you should set aside an entire room as your office, preferably one with a door, so that you can shut out distractions while you work—and shut in the mess that you don't want disturbed when you leave. If you can't afford to devote a whole room of your house, a walk-in closet or the corner of a room might do. As a last resort, there's always the dining room table after dinner has been cleared! No matter where you work, having the following two items will make the writing experience easier, more comfortable, and more inviting:

- **A comfortable chair.** Writing requires you to be seated, often for long periods, so you'll want to invest in a solid, comfortable chair. This is especially important if your computer is a stationary desktop model. You'll spend a lot of time in front of that screen, so find a chair that's height-adjustable, well padded, and ergonomically correct.

- **Decent lighting.** There's nothing like staring at a computer screen for several hours at a stretch to put tremendous strain on your eyes. To keep from squinting or having your vision become blurred, make sure you have adequate lighting.

Getting Started

Working writers don't wait for inspiration to strike; instead, they make inspiration happen by establishing a schedule up front and holding to it.

Timing and Schedules

Before writing the first words of your book, do as professional writers do: set a deadline. The following steps can help you establish a realistic timetable and target date for finishing your manuscript:

- Determine the estimated length of your book and its overall structure by creating a rough-draft table of contents and then constructing an outline or—if you are the kind of writer who finds outlines too constricting—a general summary of the plot or overriding themes. Assign approximate page lengths to each chapter based on the outline or summary you created.

- Over several days, keep track of the number of pages you complete per hour, taking into account every task that goes into their completion. For example, did you spend four hours researching a subject and two hours writing to complete the ten pages you logged on Friday? Don't be concerned about whether you are faster or slower than other writers. Whatever your pace, simply clock it and write it down; the goal of this exercise is to help you set a realistic, attainable deadline.

- Once you have established your page-per-hour pace, you can estimate the length of time each chapter is likely to take. Suppose you've been averaging three pages per hour. If you have estimated your chapter length at twelve pages, you should be able to complete the chapter in approximately four hours. Be sure that you have figured both writing and research time into your chapter calculations, or your scheduling estimates will be off. Total the number of hours you calculated for each chapter to come up with an estimate for the length of time it will take to complete your manuscript.

- Pull out your calendar and mark it with daily and weekly goals to ensure that you meet your final deadline. This is where things can get a little tricky. When you're just looking at squares on a calendar, it's easy to become overambitious and set your goals too high. Strive instead to set realistic expectations so that you will be more likely to fulfill them, which will give you a sense of accomplishment at the end of each week. Remember, these are your goals—no one else's—and they are not cast in stone. If you fall behind one week, don't panic. Simply adjust the end-date on your schedule, or catch up the following week by adding an hour or two of writing time.

- Be sure to build extra time into your schedule for those events that happen in everyone's life—expected or unexpected. If you create a cushion up front, you are less likely to end up frantically scrambling to finish during the eleventh hour.

There will always be things that threaten to get in the way of your writing. Some are legitimate—a family emergency or a crisis at work—but many are not. Do you really need to scrap your writing schedule to meet a friend for coffee on Monday night? Or, could that movie you want to see wait until the weekend? Schedules are meant to be flexible, but take care that you don't look for excuses not to write. By the same token, don't become stressed if you have to cut a writing session short through no fault of your own. If you don't meet your estimated page quota one day, you can always catch up the next.

"I make sure I spend six hours a day in front of my typewriter whether I have any ideas or not."

When you face roadblocks or become tempted to give up on your writing because it isn't going as you'd planned, just stop, take a deep breath, and remember why you started this project in the first place. Writing your book is supposed to be an enjoyable and satisfying personal endeavor. Don't let it become a chore.

When Life Gets in the Way

Few people, especially first-time authors, have the luxury of being able to write full-time. In all likelihood, you, like most authors, have to try to squeeze writing time into an already packed schedule of work and family activities. If you're trying to handle a full-time job while writing a book on the side, here are a few suggestions to help you juggle the workload:

You can write anywhere!

- **Get away…far away.** Withdraw some money from your savings account and subtract a few days from your allotted vacation time, then immerse yourself both in the splendor of being in a special, faraway place and in the luxury of having time to write. Your destination could be a cottage on the beach in The Bahamas or a rented apartment smack in the center of Paris or New York. Choose any place likely to get your creative juices flowing and to give your writing a jump-start. Just remember that wherever you go, you're not there to play full-time tourist. Your primary purpose is to work on your book.

"I need peace and quiet to concentrate. During my holiday vacation to the remote island of Rum Cay in The Bahamas, I faced a book deadline that couldn't wait. I had my laptop with me so I parked myself in a gazebo by the beach; the only things that drove me back inside were a dead computer battery and sand flies! Otherwise I got so much done—in a beautiful, calming setting where I could focus solely on writing without feeling stressed by daily pressures."

—Diane Gedymin
   Co-author, *Get Published!*

- **Get away…close to home.** Don't have the funds or time to take an out-of-town vacation? Find a library with rich oak shelves and tables. Or head for a museum where they'll let you sit for hours with your pad and pencil, writing while you bask in the beauty of wonderful works of art. Wander through a botanical garden or take a walk in the park, then claim a bench and go to work. Or just go out for coffee—almost every café now gives you the capability to connect to a server, surrounded by other highly caffeinated people working furiously on their laptops. Any place that offers an escape—whether it's one surrounded by quiet and solitude or by a busy crowd—will make you feel as though you've gotten away.

"I advise authors to experiment until they find a location that works for them. I've found that I do my best writing while working on my laptop during early morning visits to Starbucks. I draw energy from the people around me—background noise actually helps me to concentrate. With a boost from a large latte, I find I can write a first-draft chapter in just a few hours."

—Susan Driscoll
Co-author, *Get Published!*

- **Get away…at home.** If you really can't afford to go anywhere, spend a few dollars—or at least some time—to create a special writing space under your own roof. It could be a traditional office-like setting equipped with just the right desk, chair, and lighting. Or it could be a complete departure from the norm—a quiet little haven tucked into a corner behind a Japanese screen, where you burn candles and listen to inspiring music while you tap away on your keyboard. No matter what décor or space you choose, hang a Do Not Disturb sign on whatever you have for a door, and mean it! This is your special time and space; let no one disrupt it.

- **Don't let in distractions.** Just because you've carved out a great space in which to write doesn't mean your problems are over. There are still plenty of distractions to keep you from focusing on the task at hand. Do your kids disregard your Do Not Disturb sign? Hire a sitter for a few hours each week—even when you're just down the hall—to give you a chunk of uninterrupted writing time. Do the household chores threaten to become overwhelming? Arrange with your spouse to trade tasks and time, or hire some outside help.

- **Make time to write.** It's a mistake to assume that you can simply *find* time to write; you must deliberately *make* it. If your full-time job is extremely demanding—you're working overtime and then some—consider cutting back on your hours. Perhaps you could arrange to work part-time for a month or two or to take an extended leave of absence, but *only* if you won't jeopardize your job or future career prospects. Whatever you do, don't quit your day job—at least not until you become a best-selling author!

For me, writing is a discipline, much like playing a musical instrument; it requires constant practice and honing of skills. For this reason, I write seven days a week. My routine begins at around 4:00 AM every morning, when there are no distractions. By making writing my first order of business every day, I am giving it enormous symbolic importance in my life, which helps keep me motivated. If I'm not at my desk by sunrise, I feel like I'm missing my most productive hours.

—Dan Brown, Author of *The Da Vinci Code* (Doubleday), as quoted in *Times Online*, March 14, 2006 (www.timesonline.co.uk)

WRITING YOUR MANUSCRIPT

No two writers approach writing in exactly the same way. Some like to plan their books from start to finish before they sit down to write; others prefer to fly by the seat of their pants, letting the book take the lead. However, all successful writers have one thing in common: persistence.

To Outline or Not to Outline

For writers, even those with several books to their credit, there's nothing quite so intimidating as facing that first blank page. Two schools of thought exist among writers about how best to approach the task of beginning a book.

On one side are the writers who believe you should never start writing without knowing exactly where you're going to end up. They're the advocates of the outline. Before they start writing, they plan every detail of their books. If it's a novel, they carefully craft the conflict and determine character motivation; they know when the turning points will occur, what the black moments will be, and how all of it will be resolved in the end. If it's a nonfiction book, they lay out the overall structure of the book and make sure that each chapter points to the conclusion they want to draw.

On the other side of the writing community are the free spirits, those who start writing with only the kernel of an idea. They worry that an outline might be too limiting: "What if I have a great idea in the middle of writing my book and have nowhere to put it?" They're advocates of the go-with-the-flow approach to writing that doesn't depend on a lot of planning and allows them the flexibility to make radical changes in direction as they work their way from chapter to chapter.

Which is the right approach? Either. Or neither. It's up to you. This is your book, so you should write it in any way you please. Beware, though, of the *internal editor*. That's the little internal voice that tempts you to make each page perfect before you move on to the next. If you succumb to that voice, you'll end up writing and rewriting the same few pages over and over until you finally lose interest in your book and drop the project altogether.

Keep in mind that few, if any, good books have ever been printed directly from a first draft. Even the most proficient writers have to rewrite whole chapters of their books; many produce multiple drafts before they pronounce a book complete. Don't worry if what you first put down on paper isn't perfect. You can go back and fix it later. The beauty of writing on a computer is that you can add or delete material, even move entire sections around, quite painlessly. The important thing is to get the story down in the first place.

Formatting Your Manuscript

At this point in the writing process, the format of your manuscript is not nearly as important as its content. Don't worry about whether you're using the right typeface or point size. Just write! You can adjust the details, such as margins, tabs, fonts, and other style issues once you've finished writing. In upcoming chapters, you'll learn how to format your manuscript and graphics for submission to iUniverse.

Perseverance Pays

If you read the interviews with best-selling authors that regularly appear in writers' magazines, one fact quickly becomes clear. Regardless of their writing style or genre, best-selling authors share a single characteristic: they did not give up. Every successful writer has a personal tale of disappointment, but discouragement never got in the way of the work. Even in the face of multiple rejections, these authors kept chipping away. They stuck to the job and saw it through to completion. Writing isn't just about talent or desire; it's about persistence.

WORDS TO WRITE BY

You've made the decision to turn your writing dream into a reality. Now it's up to you to carry out your plans and get the job done. Here are some words of advice to help you stay the course:

- Commit to writing your book!
- Do whatever it takes to ignite your creative spark.
- Believe in yourself and your book.
- Trust your own opinions but be willing to take advice from others.
- Treat your writing career like the business it is; don't hesitate to invest the necessary time and money to make it successful.
- Take it slowly and don't give up; over time, your book will emerge.

You're a writer—now take the next step and become a published author!

Chapter 3

BOOKSTORE BROWSING

If your goals for writing are modest or personal, you may want to skip this chapter. If you hope to appeal to a larger audience, however, this chapter is a must-read.

To succeed in the marketplace, you'll need to start taking notes now—during the writing process or even before. Identify not only your audience but also your competition. Once your book is published, you'll have to compete for readers with several other professionally published books like your own. The more you know about your competition, the greater your chances of succeeding.

Browsing the shelves of your nearest bookstore is a good way to meet your competition. Don't let the word *browsing* fool you—consider a bookstore visit vital research for the success of your book, as it is the best means of assessing your competition and maximizing sales.

Although you can now casually browse online bookstores—viewing the front covers of several titles along with some descriptive copy—nothing can replace the experience of visiting a store physically and examining hardcover and paperback books. Retail bookstores provide a gold mine of information for writers beyond what they can get online. Pay attention to what's on the tables and shelves or have a casual chat with a clerk. Gathering information about the books that are selling and receiving heavy promotion will greatly improve your odds of writing a marketable book.

Do Your Homework

In many ways, buying a book is similar to buying a home. First, buyers determine the area in which they want to buy a house. Once they find an area they like, they may drive by a house for sale and maybe even walk around the exterior. If they like what they see, they may commit some time to look inside. Then they'll check out the competition—comparable houses on the market, as well as those that have recently sold. Which ones sold quickly and for the highest prices? What did the other houses look like from the inside—and out? Were they well built? Should they get an opinion from a professional inspector?

Location, Location, Location!

You can apply the same considerations to your trip to the bookstore. First, find the area in the store where you'd want readers to find your book. The genre of *fiction* or *nonfiction* isn't enough to tell prospective buyers what your book is about; you need a more focused category. If you've written a novel, is it a romance or a mystery? If it's nonfiction, is it a practical self-help book about parenting or dieting, or a narrative memoir or history? Many sections of the bookstore may apply to your book, so choose one that fits the best.

The category you choose for your book is important at every step, from the cover design, to the marketing copy, to the pitch that you'll eventually use in publicizing and promoting your book, and finally to your book's placement at both brick-and-mortar and online retailers.

In large retail chains and online sites, each section of books corresponds to a national buyer who is responsible for choosing the titles stocked in that section. Traditional publishers present a book to only one buyer, so they must choose the section and buyer that best fit each title. Authors who self-publish can use bookstore section names to help determine the appropriate genre, category, and corresponding target audience for their books.

Who Are Your Neighbors?

Just as you'd want to learn about your prospective neighbors before you bought a home, you should become acquainted with the type of person who will most likely read your book—before you publish.

Target audience is defined as a specific identification of the ideal group of customers who may buy a product. When that product is a book, identifying a target audience can help you ensure that the tone and style of both the content of the book and its look are appropriate. While a casual, chatty tone wouldn't be appropriate for a medical-school text-book, that would be the perfect style for a guide to dating. Take these two books, for example:

- *Real Women.* Target audience: females, ages thirty-five to forty-nine. They are politically minded, socially conscious women who care about current issues but don't consider themselves feminists. They are working mothers who shop at convenience and discount stores but pride themselves on being able to find bargains without sacrificing quality; they occasionally shop online. They are family-oriented but take care of themselves by exercising and eating well and have interests and hobbies of their own.

- The *Harry Potter* series. Target audience: eleven- to sixteen-year-olds—although literally *all* ages read Harry Potter books in record numbers. The book must likewise appeal to adults—specifically, parents—because they will probably be the ones who purchase the book and are often readers as well. The covers, however, are clearly aimed toward children.

CLANCY AND A CAPPUCCINO

The best way to learn about the titles your bookstore stocks is to gather a stack of competitive titles from the shelves and find a seat in the store's cafe, where you can spend time scanning them and deciding which ones you might like to read—or maybe even buy—and have a good cup of java while you're at it.

Pretend you're an average customer, or perhaps a bookstore buyer, and determine which book features matter most to you as you browse—what makes you pick the books you put in your basket. Later in this chapter, you'll find a Bookstore Checklist, along with a chart to help you answer specific questions on your visit to the bookstore, but here are some general things to think about as you get started:

- What do the covers look like? Some self-help books, for example, have bulleted lists on the front telling prospective readers exactly what they're getting between the covers. Novels, on the other hand, have shorter titles that might be more intriguing.

- When you flip through the book, does it seem easy to read? Is it filled with interesting data, charts, tables, or illustrations?

- Read the back cover. Does the copy on a novel tell you just enough about the book without revealing too much? Does a nonfiction cover tell you what you'll learn from reading the book?

- Does the author biography give you confidence in the writer's ability to write this particular book or interest you otherwise?

- What do the author photos look like? Are they taken in informal or professional settings?

- To what target audience do the books in the appropriate section for your book appeal?

- Read selections from each book to see how good it is. Does it have endorsements or reviews or maybe even a foreword by someone who's an authority on the subject?

- Most important, answer the question: how is my book different?

Readers have a huge selection of books to choose from—make sure they leave the store with yours.

When Barnes & Noble reviews a title, the quality of the book cover is critical. If the cover is unattractive, it doesn't convey to the potential reader the
genre or the message of the content. There has to be a level of sophistica-
tion and appeal present on the cover to make the customer turn the book
over to find out more. The excerpts, reviews, or bullet points of the book's
highlights on the back cover have to be intriguing enough to make people
want to open the book and read a few pages.

—Marcella Smith
   Director, Small Press & Vendor Relations
   Barnes & Noble, Inc.

TRUST THE EXPERTS

Just as you might rely on the experience and judgment of a well-respected
real estate broker, trust your bookseller. The clerk in a particular department may know a tremendous amount about that area—what the best
sellers are and why, for example. Here are a few other questions you can
ask about the best sellers in your book's genre:

- What made them sell? Did the authors promote the books?

- Did the author do any local events? If so, were they sponsored by
  local companies or organizations?

- What's hot? What isn't?

PLANTING SEEDS

If it seems appropriate, you could also discuss your own publishing goals
with the bookstore staff. Tell them about your book (a twenty-second
"elevator" pitch at the most), but be considerate of their time and listen

to what they have to say without being defensive or pushy. Here are some questions you might ask:

- Is there a need for a book on your subject? Is the idea unique?

- Can they recommend a similar book that worked?

- Is this area glutted with books, or is there a void that a fresh approach could fill?

- Are there local writers' groups, organizations, or media that might be interested in your subject?

- Are there certain times of year that books on your subject sell more than others? Does the bookstore offer any regular special promotions related to the subject of your book?

In addition, nothing endears you more to a bookstore manager than leaving with a full shopping bag. So support your local bookstore and fellow authors by buying books. Someday, you might be repaid in kind.

BOOKSTORE CHECKLIST AND CHART

Remember to take detailed notes, which you can refer to during different stages in the publishing process.

A last bit of advice: you don't have to answer all these questions in one visit. As a soon-to-be-published author, we hope you'll feel the excitement and pride of being part of the wonderful community of book publishing and want to return to the bookstore again and again. Most of all—have fun!

Note: You can download the following list of questions from iUniverse.com/getpublished. Once you have downloaded the list, print it and take it with you on your trip to the bookstore—and don't forget to take along a notepad so you have plenty of space for writing answers.

Category

1. In what area of the store would you like your book to appear?

2. Are there subsections within that area? If so, which one is right for your book? (Choose only one.)

Target Audience

1. Who do you think buys books in the section of the store in which you want your book shelved?

    a. How old are they?

    b. What gender?

    c. What lifestyle do they lead?

    d. What do they like to do?

    e. What are their literary interests?

2. How do the books written for this audience differ from other books? Do they look more or less sophisticated? Is the content different? How?

Title and Subtitle

1. What type of book titles and subtitles are common in your genre?

2. For fiction: Are they short and pithy? Or do they contain longer phrases?

3. For nonfiction: Is there a lot of copy on the front cover? Subtitles, copy lines, endorsements, bulleted lists?

Back Cover Copy

1. What does the back cover copy of similar titles in your genre include?

2. Does it include endorsements or advance quotes?

3. Does the last paragraph compel the reader to take action or promise a benefit?

4. How does the copy on a hardcover differ from that on a paperback book?

5. How long is the average copy?

Other Authors

1. How and where are the author's credentials and affiliations listed (on the cover or inside the book)?

2. What do they include and exclude?

3. What personal information is included?

4. How long is the average bio?

5. What do author photos in your genre look like? Are they informal photos taken in an author's home or yard? Or are they taken in a professional setting such as an office?

Endorsements

1. What type of quotes or excerpts from reviews are included in the books in your genre?

2. What organizational affiliations or credentials do the endorsers have?

3. Is there a foreword or preface in books similar to yours? If so, who wrote them?

Book Design

1. Is there an obvious style to the covers in your book's category?

2. Do these covers contain a lot of text, or mostly images?

3. Is there a common color used or seemingly avoided?

4. Which books caught your eye, and why?

    a. What do you like about the cover designs?

    b. What do you dislike?

    c. Are they in the same genre as your book?

    d. Do any of the covers have a look that is similar to what you envisioned for your book? If so, what about the cover reflects your idea?

5. What do the interiors of the books look like?

    a. Are they easy to read?

    b. Is the information clearly displayed?

    c. If it's nonfiction, is the information easy to follow?

    d. Does the general look fit the title and concept?

Contents

1. Carefully examine the contents of books in your genre.

2. What parts of the book are included (dedication, acknowledgments, table of contents, resource section, index)?

3. Are there many charts, tables, and illustrations?

4. What is the average length of the books?

Competition and Comparison

1. How do the other books in your genre differ from yours?

2. What do the successful books have in common?

3. How is yours different?

4. Honestly, are the other books better?

5. If so, how can you improve your book or make it unique?

Bookstore Competitor Analysis

Record critical information during your
visit to the bookstore in the chart below.

Competitive Title and Author	Publisher	Pub Date	Hardcover or Paperback	ISBN	Price	Notes

Note: You can download a copy of this chart from iUniverse.com/getpublished.
Or, use the chart to help create a template of your own, which you can take to the
bookstore.

Part 2

GET INFORMED

Chapter 4

HOW TRADITIONAL PUBLISHING WORKS

When aspiring authors such as Ernest Hemingway and F. Scott Fitzgerald were penning their first books in the early twentieth century, publishing was a fairly straightforward process and offered few options. You wrote a manuscript by hand or on a manual typewriter, if you owned one. If you had connections in the appropriate cultural or literary circles, you sent the manuscript to an editor at one of a handful of publishing houses in New York, and an elite few decided what was worthy of being read and published.

Advances in technology and distribution have given today's authors more control and more choices. But before you can fully understand the alternatives, it helps to know how the major trade publishers work.

THE BUSINESS OF TRADITIONAL PUBLISHING

When you hear the word *publisher,* you probably think about the major houses whose names you recognize and whose authors consistently show up on best-seller lists. These major firms are called *traditional* or *trade* publishers. Mostly headquartered in New York City, trade publishers produce books for a general audience rather than an academic or professional readership.

Trade publishing in the United States is a $5.2 billion industry. There were 172,000 new titles and editions published in 2005, which represents a 10 percent decline in new titles from 2004.[2] Five publishing conglomerates control more than 80 percent of book sales, and together those firms published only 23,017 titles in 2005, which was a 4.7 percent decrease from 2004. Moreover, 87 percent of retail bookstore sales in 2004 came from just 7 percent of the books published that year. Fewer than 1,200 new titles sold more than 50,000 copies each, while the vast majority of books published—a staggering 93 percent—sold fewer than 1,000 copies each.[3]

These statistics make it clear that a book that sells 10,000 copies in today's competitive marketplace is considered a success, which means traditional publishers undoubtedly lose money on a large number of the books they publish. As a result, they are forced to look to a few big hits for their major source of profits—think *The Da Vinci Code* or the Harry Potter series. To see even a reasonable return on their investment, then, traditional publishers must acquire and promote titles that have a higher probability of selling.

At traditional houses, acquisitions editors—those who decide whether to consider a book for publication—receive hundreds of queries, manuscripts, and book proposals each week. The few manuscripts they accept almost always come through highly respected literary agents. In fact, most large publishers have strict policies against accepting unsolicited manuscripts, and a majority of the manuscripts they receive end up in what's called the *slush pile*—the collection of unsolicited, unwanted, and unread manuscripts.

For those select few manuscripts that make it through acquisitions and publishing and onto bookstore shelves, the selection process continues. Ideally, the sales-publicity cycle for a new book is ninety days, but in reality a publisher may halt marketing and publicity efforts if a book

---

2   Bowker press release (New Providence, NJ: R. R. Bowker, 2005). http://www.bowker.com/ press/bowker/2005_0524_bowker.htm.

3   Nielsen BookScan, "2004 Overview," September 2005.

doesn't generate reader demand within two weeks to a month. In addition, because the publishing industry is one of the very few that accepts full returns of its products, booksellers may send unsold books back to the publisher for credit. Publishers then *remainder* books (sell off excess stock to retailers who resell them at bargain prices) that don't meet sales expectations in order to make room for upcoming titles that have more profit potential.

What does all of this mean to the new author? To be accepted by a trade publisher, a book written by an author who hasn't been previously published can't just be good; it must either be exceptional or be written by an author whose reputation or celebrity status is exceptional. The editors who work in traditional houses don't have time to make major overhauls to manuscripts or to handhold inexperienced authors who must wade through extensive revisions.

Yet, there's no question that going the traditional route can be an ideal way to debut your writing, and despite the odds, new writers who rise above the pack do still land traditional contracts. To help you overcome the odds and make informed decisions about publishing your book, here's an inside look at how traditional publishing typically works.

The Gatekeepers

Literary agents, the gatekeepers for most traditional publishing houses, assess the quality and marketability of an author's proposal or manuscript to determine whether they think it's salable to a publisher. Good agents have close working relationships with many editors and are careful to send them only quality works that they believe in as well as those they know suit a particular editor's taste or a publisher's range of categories. Agents, then, are understandably selective in accepting clients.

When a trade publisher does make an offer, the agent negotiates on behalf of the author to get the most money and the best terms for the

A Prized Rejection

Just because the publishing gatekeepers decide not to accept you and your manuscript doesn't necessarily mean there is a problem with your writing. Consider the exposé in Britain's *Sunday Times* in which type-written pages of a book published by a Booker Prize-winning author were sent to and rejected by several large publishers and literary agencies. According to the article, "Critics say the publishing industry has become obsessed with celebrity authors and 'bright marketable young things' at the expense of serious writers."[1] Although we may not know all of the considerations taken into account in rejecting the author's work, one thing is certain: modern seekers of literary talent may reject your book regardless of how well it is written. But take comfort. If you find yourself rejected by the modern traditional community, know that you are among prize-winning company.

---

1   Jonathan Calvert and Will Iredale, "Publishers Toss Booker Winners into the Reject Pile," *Sunday Times*, January 1, 2006, http://www.timesonline.co.uk/.

deal. The agent also bears responsibility for ensuring that the author agreement is in line with industry standards. Most important, because editors change houses so often in today's volatile publishing climate, an agent is often the one consistent contact authors have throughout their writing careers. An agent will often play the role of everything from cheerleader to psychiatrist, editor to lawyer, advocate to negotiator—and, in the end, the accountant who monitors sales and royalties. Moreover, reputable agents don't take a penny of their well-deserved commissions until the ink has dried on your contract, so you can trust that they'll work as hard as they can to place your book and garner the attention it deserves.

The Major Functions of Traditional Publishers

Although each traditional publisher's procedures and policies vary, most of them generally provide five major services for their authors:

- **Editorial.** Nearly every book project begins with an editor, who first acquires the title and then works closely with the author to turn a good manuscript into a great one. While authors may grumble about having to rewrite whole passages or to make even minor changes, savvy authors know their work will be better for it. The editorial process—from the big-picture editing done by in-house or acquisitions editors down to the detailed polishing done by freelance service providers—ensures that the content of the final book meets the quality standards of the publisher and industry. Good editors make authors and publishers shine.

- **Design and production.** The transformation of your computer-generated manuscript into a bound book happens in these departments. The design group creates the cover and interior design, and the production department coordinates the printing of the bound galleys, the final book, and any subsequent reprints.

- **Marketing and publicity.** Books don't sell themselves. They need a coordinated marketing and publicity effort. Marketing and publicity departments write cover copy, create seasonal catalogs for sales reps and bookstore buyers, coordinate store promotions, arrange book reviews, and—for major titles—arrange publicity and media appearances. Regardless, most publishers expect authors to actively participate in marketing. In fact, many authors, in light of the shrinking or even nonexistent publicity and marketing budgets of today's publishers, choose to hire their own publicists.

- **Sales.** Each season, the sales department is responsible for presenting books to retail store buyers. National account representatives work with large book retailers such as Barnes & Noble, Borders, Amazon.com, and national retail chains, while regional representatives call on independent booksellers and smaller retail venues. Others work only with wholesalers and distributors, who supply retailers both inside and outside the bookstore world. While the large publishing houses typically have their own sales forces, smaller publishers use commission sales representatives to call on retailers. Commission sales reps are independent agents who earn a commission on sales and usually represent multiple publishers. The number of advance orders placed by retail buyers before a book's publication is the basis for determining the quantity of titles produced on the first printing.

- **Warehousing and distribution.** The warehousing and distribution functions are usually aligned under the operations umbrella, which may also include finance, order entry, shipping, and customer service. The publisher ships printed books to its own warehouse for storage. As orders come into the warehouse, the books ship out either directly to a bookstore or, in the case of large retailers, to a regional distribution center.

How Most Traditional Publishers Choose Titles

John Steinbeck wrote, "The profession of book writing makes horse racing seem like a solid, stable business." Decades later, his wise and witty words apply even more. Selling a manuscript to a traditional publisher is anything but an exact science. Timing, perhaps even more than talent, is everything. You can write a great book on an interesting subject, but if you submit it to an acquisitions editor at an inopportune time, the publisher may not acquire it. Take, for example, the following time-sensitive scenarios:

- Your book lands on an editor's desk the week she's looking for something entirely different to round out the spring or fall list.

- The editor recently acquired a title with a similar subject or by an author who is better known.

- A glut of books on that subject already exists (even though yours is better), or was just acquired by editors at competing houses.

- A book similar to yours just hit the best-seller list.

As painful as it may be, getting a rejection letter doesn't necessarily mean your book is bad. It might only mean that your book isn't right for that particular publisher at that particular time.

Book publishing is a business, and if you are a new author, you haven't yet established a track record for sales. Frankly, you represent a risk that many editors are unwilling to take, and there's not a lot you can do to convince them otherwise. What you can do, however, is write the best book you can (about a unique or timely topic on which you are qualified); submit it to an agent or, if applicable, to a publisher; and then hope that your timing is opportune.

Follow the Rules!

Be sure to strictly follow the policies for submitting your manuscript, whether it's to an agent or to an editor at a publishing house. Remember, to publishing professionals this is a business, not a pastime; agents only make commissions on the books they sell, and editors are extremely busy and must keep the company's bottom line in mind. If a publishing house requires you to send a query first, send only a query (a letter outlining the basic premise or idea of your book and inquiring whether they're interested); if you send a manuscript, you'll waste time and money. Likewise, in houses where unsolicited manuscripts are not accepted, your manuscript—no matter how great it is—will not leave the mailroom unless it was sent by an agent and will, literally, be tossed. Cutesy tricks or gifts won't help your chances, either; on the contrary, gimmicks often irritate the recipient, who most likely will send your material straight to the trash.

Submissions and Acquisitions

If you strive to have your book traditionally published, know that you will face an often frustrating and lengthy process. The typical submissions/acquisitions process goes something like this:

1. First, you submit a query, then a proposal (an outline and sample material for nonfiction titles), or completed manuscript (usually required for fiction) to an agent in the hope of soliciting representation. Time passes—usually a few weeks or even months. If the agent's answer is yes, the agent then presents your manuscript or proposal to an acquisitions editor at a publishing house, after which you wait further for acceptance or rejection. If the agent says no, you submit your manuscript to another agent, and wait again, or...

   If you choose not to use an agent, you send a query or submit your manuscript directly to an editor at a publishing house. Although this is no longer allowed at most major houses, some university and small presses allow direct submissions. If you find a company that accepts direct manuscript submissions, you must wait for a response, sometimes for several months. If the publisher's answer is no, you send your manuscript to another editor and wait again, or...

2. If the editor likes your manuscript, congratulate yourself. But don't pop the cork on that bottle of Dom Perignon quite yet. The editor must now pass your manuscript on to the editorial board, which consists of fellow editors at the publishing house, who discuss the quality of the work. If the editorial board rejects your book, you're back to square one. If the board agrees it's good and encourages the acquisition...

3. The editor presents a recommendation to publish your book, usually to an in-house acquisitions board, which includes the publisher of the company or imprint, and sales and marketing department heads, who consider the sales potential of the book and its chances of success in the marketplace. If all agree that the book has potential...

4. A projected profit-and-loss statement for your book is prepared either by the publisher, the finance department, or the acquisitions editor—depending on the publishing house. At this point, the decision to accept or reject your manuscript comes down to dollars and cents; the publisher assesses the bottom line based on projected

earnings offset by the cost of production and sales. If the numbers look shaky, your book can still be rejected at this point. If the numbers look solid, however, the publisher will decide what to offer as an advance against royalties (see the "Advances and Royalties" breakout box) based on the projected sales, and…

5. You will receive the coveted call. One day, perhaps six months or more from the day you submitted your manuscript, you'll pick up the phone and hear your agent speak the words you've longed to hear: "We have an offer!"

Now, you can break out the bubbly.

Advances and Royalties

Royalties are the earnings that authors receive on each sold copy of their book. The royalty amount is usually a percentage of the retail price or, in some cases, the net amount received from a retailer. An *advance against royalties* is the amount the publisher gives an author in expectation of the book's total royalties.

Royalties usually range from 5 to 15 percent of the retail price depending on the format of the book—mass market paperbacks receiving smaller royalties than hardcover books, which have the highest rates. Some contracts assign royalty rates that go up as sales increase; for example, you might get 10 percent up to 5,000 copies sold, 12.5 percent up to 10,000 copies, and 15 percent thereafter. The lower rates are given at the beginning of the sales process to help publishers offset pre-production costs.

The publishing company deducts the author's earned royalties from the advance until the royalties exceed the advance paid; at this point, the book "earns out" its advance, and the author receives any additional royalties that are made. These sales are reported in royalty statements that are sent to authors according to a schedule outlined in the author agreement with the publisher.

How Titles Are Acquired (or Rejected)

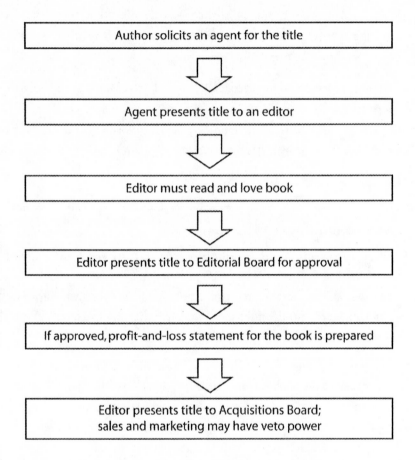

Author solicits an agent for the title

Agent presents title to an editor

Editor must read and love book

Editor presents title to Editorial Board for approval

If approved, profit-and-loss statement for the book is prepared

Editor presents title to Acquisitions Board; sales and marketing may have veto power

The Two Big Questions: Is It Good? Will It Sell?

The acquisitions process may be initiated by a great piece of writing, but it's ultimately driven by profit. Does your book have reader appeal? Will it make money for the publisher? If the answer to both these questions is yes, you've won better than half the battle.

Is It Good? Editorial Quality

Agents and acquisitions editors sometimes overlook mechanical errors in grammar and spelling if a book has what they want most—marketability. But that's not to say that you should ignore editorial quality. If you submit a manuscript that's disorganized, lacks focus, and is riddled with typos, an agent may reject it without so much as a cursory read.

If you want to get past first base with an agent or a publisher—especially as a first-time author—you must demonstrate that you know at least the basics of good writing. Because a publisher's investment is always commensurate with the anticipated return—potential sales—their editors' time is better devoted to the sure thing that a previously published writer or a truly exceptional talent represents than to the unknown potential of a first-time author.

Therefore, when considering titles, acquisitions editors first answer the basic question: is it good? Drawing on years of experience in reading books in countless genres and styles, they answer this question by first assessing big-picture issues such as organization, structure, plot, and pace and then considering the amount of time-consuming line editing that will be required.

Will It Sell? The Author Platform

In political circles, a *platform* is defined as a party's formal declaration of policy. In the publishing business, an *author platform* is defined as those qualities the author brings to the table that might directly influence book sales. In deciding which manuscripts to acquire, publishers ask the following:

- How big of an audience can the author guarantee?

- Does the author have strong credentials and a reputation in the area in which she is writing?

- Does the author have a following? Is he influential in organizations related to the topic of the book?

- Has the author appeared in any media?

- Does the author have contact with well-respected people who might write endorsements or reviews?

- Has the author already been successfully published?

- Does the author have significant Web presence through an active Web site or a blog?

- Is the author a savvy marketer who understands his target audience, knows how to reach it, and has a proven ability to convert reader interest into sales?

The answers to these and other similar questions make up the author platform.

Today I need to know your credentials, your speaking calendar, your media contacts, and whether you have an active Web site. If you want a serious book deal, those matters have to be answered in the affirmative.

—Bonnie Solow, President of Solow Literary Enterprises, Inc., as quoted in "Tips for Authors in a Sales Bind: Get a Platform" by Jeffrey A. Trachtenberg, *Wall Street Journal*, March 28, 2005.

Why the Author Platform Is Important

Even the largest retailers don't have shelf space to stock only one copy of each of the 170,000-plus books released each year, so they must be selective. The author platform is one of the key factors they consider when making that choice. Retailers look closely at an author's experience to determine whether it will be worth their while to turn over a piece of precious shelf space to a book.

The Odds of Getting Shelf Space in a Retail Bookstore

Barnes & Noble buyers consider about 60,000 titles each year for purchase and select about 40,000 to place in stores. They choose to stock many of these titles only in selected stores where sales of similar titles are strongest; for example, if books on hiking have sold well in bookstores located around national or state parks, the buyer will limit the placement of books in that genre to those regional stores, rather than placing them in all facilities nationwide.

The five major traditional publishing groups put out roughly 23,000 titles a year as of 2005, or 13 percent of the total 172,000 produced. The sales departments of these five houses have very strong working relationships with retail booksellers and national chains, so it's safe to assume that the 23,000 titles published by the five largest houses were among the 40,000 that Barnes & Noble stocked. That leaves only 17,000 titles to be chosen from the titles published by everyone else. In other words, if you're not published by a major publisher, your odds of getting stocked in a bookstore decrease dramatically.

According to the publicity director of a major literary imprint, most authors don't have a realistic basis of just how serious the competition for publicity is. "Most reviewers at major media get, on average, 300 books a week. The amount of books produced has increased while the amount of book coverage (not to mention sales) has decreased. Most authors desperately want their books to sell and would like to make livings by writing and publishing, but the sad reality is that probably 5% of authors in print are able to do that."[1]

---

1   Langer, Adam. "Enough About Me #12," June 19, 2005, http://www.thebookstandard.com/bookstandard/community/commentary_display.jsp?vnu_content_id=1000956953.

The Bookstore Stocking Model

Traditional houses rely on a well-developed publishing model, in which they print, warehouse, and distribute books before generating customer demand. This approach to bookselling, which we call the *bookstore-stocking model*, or the *distribution/demand model*, is shown below.

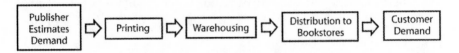

In this model, publishers *present* titles to retailers before they are even printed (and sometimes even before they're written), *distribute* the books to bookstores well before their publication dates, and then time book reviews and publicity to *create demand* for titles immediately after publication. Here's how it works.

Planning and Presentation to Retailers

Trade publishers typically start a book's publication process by determining the optimal month to release a title, then work backward to create a schedule and publishing plan that ensures they meet the target publication date. Large publishers organize the release of their books into three or four seasons per year and then slot each title into the appropriate season.

Publishers *sell* books—that is, they present books to retail bookstore buyers—months before they are published and sometimes even before the author has completed the manuscript. *Sales conferences,* in which publishers introduce the list of upcoming titles to the sales force, occur three to four months prior to the next season so that sales reps can begin soliciting orders months before publication. When calling on bookstore buyers, sales reps use a catalog that lists the titles slated for release in upcoming months. In turn, buyers use the catalog as a reference to help them make purchasing decisions.

Retailers consider five main factors when deciding whether to put a book on the shelf: (1) the book's quality; (2) its cover design; (3) the marketing and publicity plans for the title; (4) the author platform; and (5) the *track*, which is the sales history of an author's previous titles or, in the case of a first-time author, the sales of similar titles by other authors.

In short, retailers determine how many copies of a book to order based on how much demand they think the publisher and the author can generate for the title.

Examples of publishers' catalogs.

Securing Reviews and Publicity Bookings

Publicity and marketing departments begin arranging events and reviews well before a book's printing but strategically time them to coincide with the target publication date.

The publicity department works to secure newspaper and magazine stories, reviews, and—for select titles—media appearances, interviews, book signings, and other events. Once books have been typeset, the marketing and publicity departments send out advance copies of uncorrected proofs, called *galley copies* or *bound galleys*, to producers and reviewers at regional and national media outlets, book-review journals, and event planners.

The range and scope of marketing and publicity efforts for a book always depend on the assigned marketing budget. Publishers do not, for example, create galley copies of every book they publish. And publishers now pitch only the top authors to the media; automatic multiple-city author tours are a thing of the past. In fact, unless you're a best-selling author or have an exceptional media hook for your book, you'll be expected to do—and pay for—the bulk of the publicity for your book. Moreover, because of the large quantity of titles that reviewers and producers receive, they can look at only a small percentage of them, and major journals, such as *Kirkus Reviews* and *Library Journal*, give priority to reviewing titles sent by major publishers.

The Odds of Getting Your Book in a Review Journal

Kirkus Reviews, a prestigious book-review journal, publishes only 5,000 reviews each year. That means most books, even many published by major houses, do not get reviews. If you are not traditionally published, getting your book reviewed by the most prestigious review sources is unlikely.

Printing and Delivery

A traditional publisher determines the first print quantity of a title based on the number of copies retailers have ordered in advance of publication. Books are printed and shipped to the publisher's warehouse. From there, the publisher sends copies to retailers.

Major titles are shipped according to a *lay down* schedule, which means retailers nationwide receive the books on or around the same day. To ensure fair competition among titles, publishers enforce strict policies prohibiting retailers from selling a major new release before its publication date—also called the *on-sale date*.

At that point, it's up to readers to decide whether a book will become a best seller.

Bookstore Stocking, Book Sales, and Returns

Publishers hope that the concentrated media coverage that happens soon after the on-sale date will drive readers into the store and quickly accelerate sales.

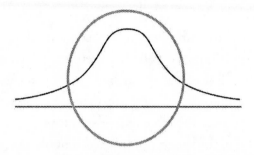

This bell curve represents the ideal hits-driven model for a traditionally published book. Publishers print a quantity of books in advance, *then* try to accelerate sales in a short time to create best sellers.

The average sales cycle for a trade book is ninety days, but most of the publicity and media coverage for a title occurs in the first two to four weeks after publication. When it comes to achieving best-seller status, a book's long-range sales do not count—only sales in a given week, relative to the sales of other books that week, matter for purposes of making the best-seller list. By squeezing publicity and media coverage into a short window of time, publishers hope to make potential customers aware of the book, drive them into the bookstore, and create enough sales velocity in a mere couple of weeks to propel the title onto regional or national best-seller lists.

Pay attention to the media—you're likely to see a review or an advertisement for a new title the same week that you see the author on several talk shows. You'll also see that same book prominently displayed in the bookstore during this period; the publisher probably paid for this placement and scheduled it to coincide with the author's major publicity exposure.

After an initial phase of orders that results from successful publicity, publishers depend on word of mouth to drive book sales further. Because most readers purchase books that have been recommended by a friend or trusted source, a majority of the ninety-day sales cycle is left up to this no-cost method of publicity (as well as to the author's own efforts).

If demand for the title doesn't materialize in those first ninety days, the game is over. Retailers send unsold inventory back to the publisher for full credit. Major publishers have been forced to build separate warehouses just to handle the volume of returns, which are, on average, 40 percent of sales but can climb as high as 60 percent for books that had great early promise but poor performance on the retail level. Most returned books are then remaindered, or sold to discounters for pennies on the dollar. Often, the largest publishers sell books in containers by the pound, and discounters who specialize in remainders don't even know which titles they are purchasing.

"As a cost-cutting measure, for our fall list we
have decided to bypass traditional bookstore sales and subsequent
remaindering, and instead go directly to the shredder."

THE REALITIES OF TRADITIONAL PUBLISHING

Given the risks and costs involved in the bookstore-stocking model of publishing, it's no wonder mainstream publishers are so selective about what they publish.

Further, the harsh realities of the industry demand that all traditional industry players—publishers, agents, retailers, and reviewers—support one another. Publishers rely on agents to present high-quality titles with potential salability. Retailers trust major publishers to select titles that will bring customers into the store and to do the marketing required to generate demand. Reviewers support publishers by adhering to their timetables (writing reviews in advance but publishing them only after the books land in the stores) and by choosing to review titles from publishers who have a track record of sending only reputable books. In turn, publishers keep in mind potential bookstore orders and reviews when they decide whether to acquire a manuscript.

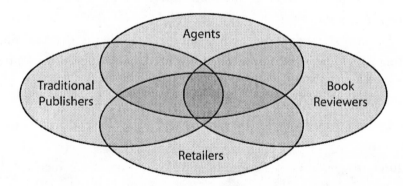

Interlocking relationships among the major players in the publishing industry.

The unfortunate result of this mutual support system is that authors generally must secure representation to break into the equation. In most cases, those authors who don't fit the formula won't get an agent and, therefore, won't be able to land a traditional book contract, get stocked nationally in retail bookstores, or garner book reviews—not to mention media exposure. Consequently, many authors find it easy to get into a negative them-against-me frame of mind regarding traditional industry players.

To avoid this unconstructive frame of mind, authors should consider that although publishers and booksellers are indeed in the business of making money, so, too, are they. Regardless of why you write—whether to inform or help others, to gain prestige among colleagues in your industry, or to express your creativity—you probably wouldn't mind also making a profit, even if that's not your sole purpose. If you put yourself on the same page with all parties involved, you'll better understand what you need to do to be successful.

THE SMALL-PRESS ALTERNATIVE

As traditional publishers have gotten more selective about the titles they publish, more small-press publishers have evolved to pick up the slack. If you are considering the small-press alternative, it pays to first understand some realities about this publishing sector.

The term *small press* can be misleading. Considering that five publishing conglomerates control four-fifths of all book sales in the United States, the majority of the nation's publishers, who lie outside that tiny circle, could be considered small. In the publishing industry, however, a small press is broadly defined as a firm that releases fewer than fifty titles per year.

Interestingly, although mergers and acquisitions have reduced the number of trade publishers, the small-press segment of the publishing market continues to grow by leaps and bounds. In 1980, about 12,000 small presses existed in the United States. By 2004, that number rose to more than 85,000.

The most successful small presses are typically niche publishers; they focus on books that fit into a specific category or cover a particular subject, and they have developed a reputation for quality publishing within that niche. Many university presses fall into this category.

The Benefits of Small Presses

Some authors prefer working with small presses, in part because these boutique publishers know and are committed to the subject matter of the books they elect to publish, and in part because they publish fewer titles per year, which enables some of them to devote more time to individual authors and books.

Unlike large publishers, which typically choose only a few high-profile books on their lists to heavily promote each season, small presses usually give more attention to all. And, as mentioned earlier, small houses are more apt to consider unsolicited manuscripts, which major houses will not.

There can also be a certain cachet to publishing your book with a small press, especially one that carries the name of a prestigious educational institution, one that is considered an influential organization within your field, or one that is well-known for quality publishing within a particular niche.

The Drawbacks of Small Presses

The publishing services offered by small presses are somewhat limited. First, the fact that these houses publish far fewer books per year than traditional publishers do doesn't guarantee that their editors have more time to devote to manuscripts. In fact, the opposite may be true: small presses have smaller staffs, which means their editors often are under even greater time constraints than the editors who work for major publishers.

Second, unless your small press has an excellent reputation for producing a specific category of books, it's unlikely your title will be stocked in many bookstores or widely reviewed. While trade publishers have their own sales forces made up of reps who have powerful relationships with retailers, small presses usually share a commission sales force with other small presses and lack the clout of the major players. Consequently, books published by many small presses get little—if any—retail shelf space.

In short, unless you're publishing with a mid-sized or larger publisher, or unless you're working with a small publisher with a proven track record, don't expect to achieve dramatic sales or significant earnings through the bookstore-stocking model.

What to Watch for When Choosing a Small Publisher

Horror stories abound about small-press publishers who exploit authors. If you grant any publisher—small or large—an exclusive license to publish your book for the term of the copyright or for any lengthy period, make sure they pay for all reasonable expenses associated with publishing your book, from editing to distribution. If a publisher doesn't have the means to invest in your work before it is published, they might not have the means to pay you royalties after the fact.

Similarly, be wary of publishers that demand that you buy a large quantity of books from the first printing. Some companies, under the pretense of being a traditional publisher, label this type of contractual relationship a *co-venture*, sometimes paying the author as little as $1 while requiring thousands of dollars from authors in return.

You should also make sure that the small press has the means to market and distribute your book to both bookstore and non-bookstore retailers. Reputable small presses usually have a relationship with a *distributor*—a company that has its own sales force that handles advance sales, warehousing, order fulfillment, and returns processing.

To ensure that yours is the kind of book that the sales reps will understand and be able to pitch properly, ask to see the publisher's retail catalog featuring upcoming and backlist titles. You could also ask for the names of other publishers their distributor represents; researching them online will give you an idea of the range of titles and publishers represented by the small press's distributor. If your book is compatible with the types of books being sold, your title may be a good match for this particular small press.

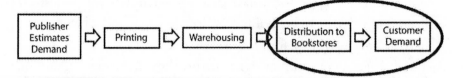

The bookstore-stocking model. When considering a small press, make sure
the publisher has a specific plan for advance selling and distribution to
bookstores, and for marketing to generate customer demand.

What to Watch for in a Small-Press Contract

If you are offered a small-press contract, and you don't have an agent,
seek legal advice to ensure that the contract is up to industry standards.

Some agents are also attorneys, and those who are not either have a
lawyer on retainer or are familiar enough with the legalities of the publishing business to protect your rights and get you everything to which
you are entitled. Good agents never allow publishers to build in terms
that are not customarily accepted in the industry. In addition, although
the best contract terms typically go to the best-selling authors, a reputable agent will go to bat for even the most unseasoned writer.

Most small publishers are legitimate in this respect and use industry-
standard contracts; however, some are unprofessional and even unscru-
pulous, run by people who publish as a hobby rather than as a business
but who nevertheless tie up your rights. If you hire a lawyer who has
experience with book-publishing precedents, you will have to pay legal
fees up front, but these will protect your rights throughout the term of
the copyright.

One negotiating point that often becomes a hot-button issue has to
do with who owns both the publication rights to your book and subsidiary rights such as foreign language translation and, especially, film
rights. Whereas publishers want to secure as many rights as possible,
for as long as possible, and for as little an investment as possible, writers
and their agents are necessarily concerned about relinquishing unlimited
rights to the publisher.

A good literary agent or contract lawyer familiar with the publishing industry knows what rights publishers usually retain and what the customary arrangements are for fairly sharing the revenues of the sale of such rights. For example, film rights are usually retained by the author, whereas book-club rights never are; on the other hand, translation rights, called *foreign rights*, can go either way.

Reality Check

If you are set on publishing the traditional way—submitting a manuscript to an agent or editor—consider the statistics.

- Fourteen million adult Americans engaged in some form of creative writing last year.[1]

- Finished manuscripts for an estimated 8 million novels and 17 million how-to books are lying in desk drawers all over the country, waiting to be published.[2]

- Between 1982 and 2002[3]

  o the number of adults reading literature *declined* by 10 percent, which represents 20 million fewer readers.

  o the number of creative writers *increased* by 30 percent, which represents 3 million more writers against whom you might potentially compete.

---

1   National Endowment for the Arts, *Reading at Risk: A Survey of Literary Reading in America,* Research Division Report No. 46 (Washington, DC: National Endowment for the Arts, 2004), p. 4. http://www.arts.gov/pub/ReadingAtRisk.pdf.
2   Marilyn and Tom Ross, "Book News, Publishing Industry Statistics and Self Publishing Facts," http://www.selfpublishingresources.com/Booknews.htm.
3   *Reading at Risk,* pp. 21, 22.

Be careful about the rights you give up, but don't be overly restrictive. If you don't have a lawyer or an agent, and you have limited experience in this area, it may be preferable to let the publisher retain control—if they have a staff member on board who is experienced in selling various types of rights. However, don't neglect to address the following two items and to negotiate them, if necessary: (1) find out how the revenues will be divided and ensure they are shared fairly and according to common industry practice, and (2) be sure that your contract includes a termination clause that enables you to get your rights back if the publisher doesn't sell at least three hundred copies in a year.

Even with the increased number of small presses, the odds of getting a book contract are not in your favor. And the odds of getting stocked in bookstores with the traditional advance-stocking model are even lower. Luckily, there is a model that puts the author in control of the publishing process and eliminates the risks and barriers of the traditional stocking model—self-publishing.

In a retail world increasingly dominated by national bookstore chains, it's hard to sell books by new authors without a track record. I often say to these people, "You should try self-publishing first, get yourself known on Web sites and start building an audience and sales; when you have it, come back, because then we can make the case that we can get you out in a big way."

—Mark Gompertz, Publisher of Fireside and Touchstone (divisions of Simon & Schuster), as quoted in "The Book Business: How to Be Your Own Publisher" by Sarah Glazer, *New York Times*, April 24, 2005

Chapter 5

BREAKING THE BARRIERS

The traditional bookstore-stocking model works—for books by celebrities and established authors who already have a platform or track record, or for those rare, extraordinary books that an entire publishing staff rallies behind, making it the buzz of the business.

If your book doesn't fit into one of those categories, you need a different model—one that bypasses traditional industry players and allows you to publish and market directly to your readers. The do-it-yourself movement, now firmly rooted in music and film, is becoming equally popular in book publishing. Advances in technology, together with the speed and accessibility of the Internet, make it possible for you to professionally publish your book, find your target audience, and develop a platform to reach readers. Quite literally, you can do it yourself.

THE DO-IT-YOURSELF MOVEMENT

The do-it-yourself (DIY) movement is all about *disintermediation*. Disintermediation, or operating without an intermediary or middleman, is a concept that's catching on among creative types worldwide—particularly in the film and music industries. Independent filmmakers showcase their work across the world at prestigious events such as the Sundance and Tribeca film festivals. In fact, many of today's most highly acclaimed films started as independent productions, called *indies*. Likewise, indie musicians and bands who aren't recorded and distributed on major labels are now at the forefront of the newest sounds to hit the charts, and they showcase their talents in similarly acclaimed music festivals such as Coachella and SXSW. Artists in both these industries have found success by using methods that bypass traditional gatekeepers to help them reach their audiences directly.

Now, finally, the DIY movement is attaining equal popularity in the book-publishing industry. Aspiring authors are breaking down the barriers of the traditional model, which relies on gatekeepers such as agents, acquisitions editors, reviewers, and booksellers to decide whether a book can get published and reach readers.

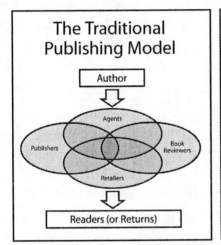
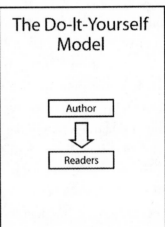

Paths between authors and readers in traditional publishing
and do-it-yourself publishing.

SELF-PUBLISHING

The DIY model in the book-publishing industry is called *self-publishing*. To self-publish is to eliminate the middleman and reach readers directly. You can start and end your self-publishing experience with a single book, produce several titles, or, as others have done, earn the opportunity to sell a traditional house the rights to your self-published book. Regardless of your self-publishing experience, the bottom line is that *you* are in control.

Of course, just as the indie film and music artists must do, as a self-publisher you must foot the costs of producing and marketing your book. The upside is that, as a self-published author, you are guaranteed to get your book published, reach your audience, and create your own success.

If all goes according to plan, self-publishing can be an extremely rewarding and potentially lucrative endeavor. A star example of this is James Redfield, author of the best seller *The Celestine Prophecy*, a story of spiritual enlightenment that reads like a fairy tale. To initially generate demand for his self-published parable, Redfield launched a full-time lecture career related to his book's topic and gave away 1,500 copies in the hope that a few satisfied readers would tell others. They did. Word of mouth created enough momentum that Redfield's book caught the attention of the traditional publishing industry, landing him an enormous advance from Warner Books. *The Celestine Prophecy* became a mega-best seller—but not before Redfield and his wife had personally sold more than 100,000 copies.

When Richard Nelson Bolles self-published the original *What Color Is Your Parachute?* in 1970—a guide for fellow clergy considering a switch to secular careers—he probably never dreamed that his hard work would pay off as well as it did, or for as long. The book became one of the top-selling career-counseling handbooks of all time and is still on the shelves in an updated edition thirty-five years later. The book is now published by Ten Speed Press and still sells several thousand copies per week.

Another example of a hugely successful self-published title is *The Christmas Box,* a touching story of twin tragedies by Richard Paul Evans. The family and friends to whom Evans gave the first few copies he had printed and bound raved about the book so much that he decided to approach several publishers; every one of them turned it down. Undaunted, Evans and his wife used their savings to publish the book themselves, and worked relentlessly to get the word out. The rest is publishing history. The title became successful enough to land Evans an advance of over $4 million from Simon & Schuster for the original title and its sequel. Evans has been a best-selling author ever since.

Robert's Rules of Order, Bartlett's Familiar Quotations, The One Minute Manager, Leadership Secrets of Attila the Hun, and *Conversations with God* all began as self-published books, and there is certainly room at the top for more.

For anyone who has the time and financial resources—and commitment—to make it happen, self-publishing is, more than ever before, a viable option. There are now two types of self-publishing available to authors who choose to do it themselves—self-publishing completely on your own and supported self-publishing.

Self-Publishing on Your Own

If you decide to publish your manuscript on your own, instead of turning your book over to a publisher, you *become* the publisher and do the bulk of the work yourself: find and hire editors, designers, and a printer to create the finished book; oversee its sales and distribution; and drive its marketing.

"I'm self-published."

The Requirements of Self-Publishing on Your Own

Entire books have been devoted to teaching authors how to go about self-publishing a book. But before you head to the bookstore to buy one of these, you should know a little about what's involved so you can decide whether self-publishing is a road you want to take. Here are some key steps you'd need to take to become your own publisher:

- **Purchase a block of ISBNs that identifies your company imprint.** An ISBN, or International Standard Book Number, is the thirteen-digit number you see on every book that identifies its title, edition, binding, and publisher. You can't buy just one ISBN; they are sold in blocks of ten. All book retailers, wholesalers, and distributors order and track books by ISBN, so every book published *must* have one unless you don't intend to sell it in stores or through online retail outlets.

ISBN stands for International Standard Book Number. Every book sold through retail channels has a unique ISBN. The first digits of the ISBN define the publisher of the book; the 0-595 prefix identifies this book as one published by iUniverse. When you fully self-publish, you need to purchase a block of ten ISBNs and establish a name for your company. You'll have to pay over $200 just to purchase your ISBNs.

- **Hire editorial service providers to give your book a professional polish.** Writers write and editors edit. No matter how capable a writer you may be, authors are just too close to their books to spot errors, and friends and relatives who volunteer to help typically don't have professional experience editing books. Whether your book is traditionally published or self-published, the key question is always the same: is it good? Although it's essential that you hire a professional book editor to, at the very least, look for spelling and grammar errors that can make a book seem amateurish, if you truly want your book to be as *good* as it can be, you will need to get an experienced book editor to help you. In addition, because even the best editors and typesetters make some mistakes, it's also important to hire a professional proofreader, after your book has been typeset and formatted, to give it a final check.

- **Hire specialists to transform your pages into a professional-quality, print-ready manuscript.** Books don't magically go from typewritten manuscripts to bound copies. To produce a book typically requires a number of people with specialized experience. If you have a better-than-average eye for design and familiarity with desktop publishing software, you may be able to handle much of the preprint preparations yourself. Be sure to carefully study competing books in your genre, however, to be certain that your book meets industry standards of quality and style. Otherwise, to create a professional-looking book, you will need to hire a cover designer, an interior designer, and a production staff experienced in book-making. This takes time, money, and, most importantly, contacts. Moreover, once you have found service providers to help you, it's difficult to always determine whether they are experienced, professional, and reputable. If you go this route, make sure to get references—and check them.

- **Decide on a printer and determine the initial print run.** Once you have your book in final preprint format and have determined how many copies you want to print, shop around. Present your material to several printers for bids. Be sure to give each one the same specifications so that you can accurately compare the estimates. In evaluating the bids, don't just look at the bottom line. Once you've narrowed it down, make sure you choose a printer that guarantees delivery dates as well as one that you trust and feel comfortable working with.

- **Prepare the final production files.** After you have a designed book and cover, you'll need to make sure your files are technically compatible with the printer you choose; for example, the printer may need to see guide marks in the margins of the pages you create and will probably require that files be prepared by experienced typesetters using professional prepress software, such as QuarkXpress, Adobe FrameMaker, or InDesign. You'll have to attend to myriad details, as well, such as creating a bar code for the back cover that allows a retailer to scan your ISBN and list price. Or, again, you can find and hire service providers to do the work for you.

- **Develop a plan for distributing and storing your book.** Many self-published authors attempt to follow the bookstore-stocking model of distribution. The reality, however, is that unless you have a great author platform, established credentials, and a marketing plan, getting a contract with a major distributor is highly unlikely and difficult at best. Most independent distributors with strong retail connections are extremely selective about the titles they represent. To convince a distributor to take on your book, you will have to present a professional book and cover *and* the marketing plan to sell it. If the distributor agrees to handle your book, it will have to compete for sales force time with titles from other small presses and self-published authors. In addition, traditional retail distribution doesn't come cheap: distributors usually require a 30 percent commission plus stocking, warehousing, and returns-processing fees.

If money is tight, you can handle the distribution yourself, but not without expending a lot of time and effort. As a self-distributor, you will have to fulfill all of your orders and devise policies regarding returns and damaged copies. You also will need to pay for storage and insurance costs for your unsold copies, unless your garage or cellar is large enough to hold several cartons of books and dry enough to prevent moisture damage. Even then, mice and bugs can get inside the cartons, or the roof could leak. Books are fragile.

Distributors vs. Distribution

Distribution is one of the most elusive terms in publishing. Getting your book into distribution means making it available for retailers to order through their systems, either directly from you or through a wholesaler. Large publishers handle their own distribution; smaller publishers rely on distributors.

Distributors are companies that customarily handle inventory, warehousing, and distribution to retailers and have a sales force to present those titles to retail buyers. Distributors generally earn a commission on every book sold and often charge additional fees for processing returns, fulfilling orders, and managing inventory.

If you self-publish using traditional printing methods, and you intend to land shelf space in bookstores, you'll need a distributor to sell, warehouse, and distribute copies of your book. The distributor will list your book in the catalog it provides to its sales reps and retailers.

Be wary of any distributor that offers you sales representation to bookstores for a fee. Reputable distributors work on commission and will represent your book only if they believe retailers will stock it (and retailers will stock your book only if you have reliable credentials and a solid marketing plan). In the end, commercial success is up to you.

- **Market your books to generate demand.** Just because a book is available for distribution doesn't mean it will sell. As a self-publisher, you will be responsible for generating reader demand for your book. That can encompass everything from paid advertising and media interviews to public speaking engagements and book signings at retail outlets. The cost for all of this promotional activity will be your responsibility.

Advantages of Self-Publishing on Your Own

- Self-publishing on your own eliminates the barriers of the traditional publishing industry.
- It is available to anyone with time and financial resources.
- It gives the author full control of the process and of the publishing rights.
- If you're successful, you can make more money.

Drawbacks of Self-Publishing on Your Own

- If you haven't done it before, the logistics and details of publishing can be overwhelming.
- Self-publishing completely on your own can be very expensive—count on an up-front investment in editing, book design, production, inventory, and warehousing.
- If you store books, beware of mice, insects, and moisture; books are easily damaged.
- The publishing and distribution aspects require a substantial investment of time and extensive resources.
- Unless you find a major distributor, your book will not get into bookstores.
- Book reviewers and newspapers will not consider reviewing self-published books, because there are already too many traditionally published books to review.

"Real" Self-Publishers

Some proponents of self-publishing firmly believe that if you don't do it all yourself, you're not a "real" self-publisher; that if you don't make the hefty financial investment needed to go it alone, you're not as committed as one who does; and that if you don't form your own company with ISBNs in your name, you're not *really* a self-publisher.

Those ideas may sound okay in theory, but the reality is that merely having more time, money, and contacts than the average aspiring author doesn't necessarily make one a better writer or a more legitimate player in the marketplace. Most people today have busy lives, limited budgets, little or no access to experienced service providers, and questions about their desire, or ability, to market aggressively—but that doesn't make them any less dedicated to the quality and success of their books or writing careers, or their books any less worthwhile. If this describes your situation, then you are a good candidate for *supported self-publishing* through iUniverse.

Supported Self-Publishing through iUniverse

At iUniverse, one of the leading providers of supported self-publishing services, we offer authors an easier and more affordable way to get published—supported self-publishing. The core difference between self-publishing completely on your own and getting support from iUniverse is that instead of having to track down and pay exorbitant prices for a host of service providers, you can allow us to provide the services for you at a cost that is considerably lower. With supported self-publishing, you do give up some of the control you'd have in full self-publishing, but only in exchange for less hassle and expense.

Like a traditional publisher, iUniverse assigns your title an ISBN, handles the logistics of your book's design, makes arrangements for printing, manages the distribution, establishes the book's selling price, sets discount rates and retail terms for booksellers and wholesalers, and pays you a royalty on each sale. You're not burdened with searching and checking references for reputable service providers to help you edit, design, and produce your book, and you're not obligated to pay high rates for their expertise. At iUniverse, you can draw guidance from an existing pool of professional book-publishing experts at an affordable price.

Unlike a traditional publisher, however, iUniverse gives you more control. You say when you're ready to publish. You choose whether you want to invest time and money in editorial services. You decide whether you want assistance to market and publicize your book. And you—not agents and editors—give the final approval of your manuscript and cover design. In addition, you control the rights to your book, so you always have the option to move to a traditional publisher or to full self-publishing once your book builds momentum.

Supported self-publishing through iUniverse also enables you to test your marketing abilities and learn about the publicity process without emptying your bank account. And because you won't have to worry about details such as typos and typefaces or distribution and warehousing, you can get back to doing what you do best—writing. Going with iUniverse may not be the right long-term solution for all authors, but for most new authors, it's the most efficient and affordable way to get started and, ultimately, *get published!*

One New York literary agent, Harvey Klinger, who recently advised a best-selling author to publish her latest novel with iUniverse after it was rejected by several New York houses, had the following to say: "The self-publishing route has become a viable alternative for a lot of these authors who can't conveniently categorize what they're doing. With the trend toward publishers consolidating, the number of houses where authors can seek out bids is also diminishing; I think the growth of iUniverse and small-press publishing is a direct result."

—Harvey Klinger quote from "The Book Business: How to Be Your Own Publisher" by Sarah Glazer, *New York Times,* April 24, 2005

Advantages of Supported Self-Publishing through iUniverse

- Publishing with iUniverse is hassle-free. We do all the cover design, book design, production, printing, and distribution work for you.

- We're fast. You can get books in around thirty to ninety days after you submit your manuscript in final form.

- You maintain control over the content and design of your book.

- We draw editorial service providers from the same pool as traditional publishers do, and we offer the same full range of services—so you get quality work from proven industry editors.

- The contract is nonexclusive, so you control your own copright and can always choose to self-publish completely on your own or sign a contract with a traditional publisher; all you need to do is give us a thirty-day notice so that we can clear the bookselling channels.

- iUniverse makes your book available through Barnes & Noble.com (www.bn.com), Amazon.com, and other online retailers.

- Your book is automatically listed in *Books in Print*.

- Your book will be available through Ingram and Baker & Taylor, the two largest book wholesalers.

- Your book can be ordered directly by customers, libraries, or bookstores through the iUniverse Web site or through our customer service department.

- You can purchase quantities of your book at significant discounts and resell them on your own.

- There are absolutely no minimum quantities; because books are printed on demand—and can be printed in quantities as little as one at a time—there is no need for warehousing and no possibility of damage.

- Publishing with iUniverse costs a fraction of what it would cost to fully self-publish—approximately $1,000 or less versus $10,000 or more.

- Because books are produced on demand and not warehoused, there are no returns.

Disadvantages of Supported Self-Publishing through iUniverse

- When you self-publish through iUniverse, your ISBN will have the iUniverse prefix rather than a prefix that designates you as the publisher.

- iUniverse pays you a royalty of 20 percent of net revenues from book sales, whereas with full self-publishing you earn whatever profits you generate after paying production, printing, and distribution costs.

- iUniverse offers different retail terms and policies than traditional publishers do. Retailers receive a lower discount on most titles, although authors have the choice of selecting a lower royalty rate in exchange for a higher retail discount. In addition, iUniverse books are not returnable.

- As you'll learn in the next chapter, producing books using print-on-demand technology necessitates slightly higher cover prices than printing methods used by traditional publishers.

WHY PAY TO BE PUBLISHED? FIVE GOOD REASONS

We've presented the advantages and disadvantages of all of the publishing options available to authors today: traditional publishing with a major house or a small press as well as both self-publishing alternatives—doing it completely on your own and supported self-publishing. In summary, here are at least five good reasons why self-publishing—paying to be published—may be your best option either now or at some point in your future.

Reason One: You Can Get to Market Faster

Going the traditional route, it could take several years to get your book published. If your book covers a time-sensitive topic tied to current events or trends, traditional publishers are more apt to reject it because they know that by press time, the hot topic you started with will have become yesterday's news. If you self-publish, you can get your book into the marketplace far more quickly.

Reason Two: You Can Control the Finished Product

A business tenet that holds true in book publishing is that the person who pays is the person in control. The amount of control you have over your book's publication process can range anywhere from very little to nearly complete. The difference lies in whether you go with a traditional publisher, choose supported self-publishing, or opt to publish completely on your own.

For Amy Fisher, the choice was easy. As you may recall, Fisher, at age sixteen, made headlines in 1992 as the "Long Island Lolita" for shooting her lover's wife. When she completed writing her second memoir, in which she describes the personal events that surrounded the crime, Fisher instructed her agent not to go the traditional publishing route. She turned instead to iUniverse.

According to an April 2005 article in the *New York Times*, Fisher's choice was all about control. She and her co-author, Robbie Woliver, knew the book would sell well, and they wanted to retain as much of the resulting profits as possible. They were right: the book landed on the *New York Times* best-seller list immediately after publication.

But Fisher had another reason for choosing to self-publish: when news of the shooting had surfaced, the media had featured sensational and not always accurate accounts of the high-profile case; despite the tragic circumstances, her relationship with Joey Buttafuoco had been fodder for countless late-night talk-show jokes. When she was ready to publish *If I Knew Then*, Fisher, who in the intervening decade and a half had served her jail time and become a wife, a mother, and a columnist, was determined not to let the media control her image again. So she turned to iUniverse, which allowed her to take full control of both the book's content and her marketing campaign. Her campaign included national and regional advertising and media interviews on countless national television and radio shows, including a full hour on *Oprah*.

Many authors prefer self-publishing for the control it offers because:

- They don't want their rights tied up for the full term of copyright (life of the author plus seventy-five years), which is the standard in traditional industry author contracts.

- They need deadlines that are more flexible than what a traditional publisher can offer.

- They want to have the final say over their books' content and covers.

- They are unwilling to allow a third party, whether it's an agent or a publisher, to act as a gatekeeper between their work and their readers—a concept known as disintermediation.

Reason Three: You Can Reach Readers Directly

As discussed at the beginning of this chapter, the book-publishing industry is one of the few remaining creative industries that has failed to fully embrace disintermediation. Although authors themselves are at the forefront of this do-it-yourself movement, it's hardly surprising that the traditional industry gatekeepers (as shown in the chart at the beginning of this chapter) still control most of what's available in brick-and-mortar stores.

Authors who pay to publish their work have the opportunity to remove these barriers to directly finding and reaching their readers. In the same way the Internet has made it possible for musicians to reach their audiences without input from the recording industry, do-it-yourself publishing can put authors directly in touch with their readers through online retailers and other innovative sales venues, bypassing traditional publishing outlets and bookstores. The fact that Amazon.com is the third largest bookseller proves that an author can reach readers without ever being stocked in a brick-and-mortar store. By circumventing the gatekeepers in traditional publishing firms, authors can reach new audiences and have an immediate and wide-ranging impact.

Reason Four: Your Success Is Determined by Your Readers

Publishers don't make books into best sellers; they just facilitate the publishing and marketing process. Your book's commercial success ultimately depends on readers. Although publicity and good reviews can go a long way toward building awareness of a new book, word of mouth is what makes it sell. One reader tells another reader, who tells another. Family members share copies among themselves. Coworkers discuss a lively page-turner or a useful reference book over lunch or coffee. And people gather at the virtual water coolers of the computer generation—Internet groups and chat rooms—to share notes on what's new, useful, or thought-provoking in the books they've read.

Just as audiences can turn an actor into a celebrity, readers can turn an author into a star. The key is to make contact with those readers—and the most direct way to do that is by self-publishing.

Reason Five: Your Investment Guarantees a Finished Book

No matter what publishing route you take, it's going to cost you money. Self-publishing guarantees results in the form of a finished book.

Traditional publishing doesn't offer such a guarantee. You'll spend the same amount of time and energy writing your book, but when you submit your book to a traditional house or agent, you will have to pay for copies, postage, and possibly even editing if an agent requires you to improve your manuscript before agreeing to represent you.

Authors who sign with traditional publishers often pay for editorial services prior to submitting their final manuscripts for acceptance, since a contract may be terminated if the editor feels the final manuscript needs too much work to become publishable. Moreover, depending on the terms of your contract, you may have to return the advance if the book is not accepted—even if you've already spent it.

If your traditionally published book makes it all the way into print, in most cases, you'll also need to invest money to make sure it sells. Trade publishers aggressively market and publicize only their best-selling authors, while first-time or unproven authors get short shrift. That means you'd need to either spend your own time and money marketing the book or hire a publicist to do it for you.

Depending on your goals and your budget, it might make better sense to put your dollars toward supported self-publishing, where you're guaranteed to have a published book in the end.

When Should You Pay to Be Published? Seven Good Scenarios

You now know *why* paying to be published is not only acceptable but, in some cases, preferable. But *when* is it the right choice? It's certainly not in every author's best interest to pay to be published. On the contrary, if you can land a book contract with an advance—that is, if someone *pays you* for the privilege of publishing your book—and it's with a reputable house that offers you an industry-standard contract, there's little reason to consider alternatives.

However, there are some scenarios in which paying to be published may be the best choice. Here are seven ideal situations for choosing supported self-publishing:

1. You designed your book as a professional tool to help you gain personal or professional recognition, to make the general public aware of your specialty, or to help you land and promote speaking engagements.

2. You want to become a traditionally published author but are having trouble getting started, and you know that by getting your book out, you can prove you have an interested readership.

3. You targeted your book for a specific niche market or a specialized audience.

4. You're interested in developing or testing your marketing skills, and you would like opportunities to experiment with a range of marketing and publicity strategies to give you a feeling for what works and what you enjoy doing most.

5. You wrote your book to appeal to a small readership that consists mainly of family, friends, or colleagues.

6. You simply want to produce a professionally published book.

7. The traditional house that originally published your book has let it go out of print.

If you are publishing for any of these reasons, you can ensure that the process is as efficient and cost-effective as possible by going with a supported self-publisher that uses a revolutionary print technology called *print-on-demand* (POD). As you'll learn in the next chapter, POD has created a new and different model of publishing, one that offers new opportunities to produce, print, and sell books in a manner that is more efficient and economical than ever.

Is It Vanity?

Some critics think that if an author pays to be published, it's vanity publishing—a term that implies that only people with giant egos, deep pockets, and self-centered intentions would consider alternatives to traditional publishing.

When the term *vanity publishing* was coined in the 1950s, here's how it worked: if an author couldn't get a traditional publishing contract, the only choice was to pay dearly to have a book published and printed. You'd send the publisher your manuscript, and for a fee of thousands of dollars, you'd receive several cartons of bound books, which you'd store in a cellar or garage and give away to a few friends and family members. The typical vanity publisher provided little or no editorial assistance, and certainly no help with marketing, sales, or distribution. Authors, therefore, were truly pretending to be published.

For the majority of authors who publish through iUniverse, *vanity* couldn't be further from the truth. As you saw earlier, there are many good reasons why an author might pay to be published and many times when it's the best choice. Let's revisit those best-case scenarios from a different perspective by asking this question: is it vanity?

- **Early market success.** iUniverse helps launch many first-time authors who lack the platform or track record to land a traditional publishing contract but who have the drive and determination to prove they can succeed. Once their books start to sell, agents and editors notice, and the books are often acquired by traditional publishing houses. These authors are clearly not vain—during their early efforts or after they've earned success.

- **The realities of the book business.** Numerous iUniverse authors have written high-quality books that are represented by literary agents—but the reality of publishing today is that even getting an agent is no guarantee of getting acquired by a traditional publisher. Fifteen years ago, the chances were far better. Just because the industry has changed doesn't mean that authors who self-publish are vain—they're savvy.

- **Speed to market.** Certain subjects date quickly. A great many iUniverse authors have ideas for books that just can't wait for the length of a traditional publishing cycle to get into the marketplace—typically a year or more from the delivery of a completed manuscript to publication. Making the most of a publicity opportunity or giving readers more information on a hot topic is good business—not vanity.

- **Late-market sales.** Very few books have sales that last forever. No matter how good or successful a book may be, there will likely come a time when the sales of that book are too low to be kept in print by its original publisher. Authors who want their books available to interested readers are not vain. iUniverse is proud to be the exclusive partner for Authors Guild, Harlem Writer's Guild, and AJSA members who want to bring their out-of-print titles back to market—these professional writers' associations obviously agree.

- **Small audiences.** iUniverse publishes many important books that have a well-defined but very small audience. These books would unlikely generate enough profit to be commercially appealing to traditional publishers, but they do appeal to the targeted audiences for whom they are written. Various war veterans and survivors of war crimes or oppression, for example, have self-published their memoirs through iUniverse. Surely, the majority of these very personal books will never be stocked on retail bookstore shelves, but it is nevertheless important that these stories are preserved as a legacy—if only for friends and family. Likewise, people who have overcome personal obstacles have come to iUniverse not out of vanity, but out of the desire to help others.

- **The realities of life.** Many authors aren't ready or able to meet the high level of commitment that traditional publishing requires. With full-time jobs and family responsibilities, these authors can't write to meet deadlines and don't have the time to engage in full-time marketing. Self-publishing through iUniverse gives these authors—who are both talented and committed to the craft of writing—a chance to find an audience on their terms and on a schedule that works for them. These authors aren't vain—they're realistic.

- **Financial status.** Some people feel that publishing completely on your own by creating a publishing company is the only legitimate way to self-publish. On the contrary, being able to afford thousands of dollars to name your own publishing company does not make your efforts more real—nor does it make you a better writer.

iUniverse isn't a *vanity* publisher—it's a *democratic* publisher. And, as anyone can tell you, democracy isn't perfect. Giving *all* authors the freedom to publish and the control to make publishing decisions means that many titles will not meet the standards of the traditional publishing industry. At iUniverse, we try to educate authors and remind them that their goals need to be in sync with their ability to invest time and money in editorial and marketing services—through iUniverse or through their own independent service providers. The more ambitious your goals, the greater the investment needed to achieve them. There are no shortcuts or quick roads to commercial success. It's not vanity to work hard and invest in your writing career— for many serious authors, it's absolutely the right choice.

WHAT AUTHORS HAVE TO SAY

After completing my biography of Stepin Fetchit, I discovered myself in competition with Pantheon Press's soon-to-be released Goliath on the same subject. I knew that the traditional publishing timeframe wouldn't work for me. My decision to publish *Shuffling to Ignominy* with iUniverse was an excellent one. The entire process was speedy and efficient, resulting in a highly professional product I was proud of. Despite the competition, my book received major reviews in both the *New Yorker* and the *New York Times*. I've now been contacted about turning *Shuffling to Ignominy* into a documentary film. If I hadn't gone with iUniverse, none of this would have happened.

—Champ Clark
    Author, *Shuffling to Ignominy*, and correspondent, *People* magazine

I have had twelve books published by mainstream houses including Simon & Schuster and Dell. My writing has also appeared in the *New York Times, Newsweek,* and other magazines. That is to say, I am a professional writer with a lot of experience in publishing. But I have to tell you that after having my second book published with iUniverse, I'm hooked. I cannot imagine going back to the commercial houses. Naturally, most authors would rather be paid than have to shell out money to get a book to market. Me too. On the other hand, all the benefits—total creative control over the project, a lightning-fast production process, a great-looking book, and even the chance to pay for extra support if possible—do not exist in the mainstream at all, and they are well worth the trade-off.

—Alan Robbins
Author, *A Small Box of Chaos*

I now have an agent who is pitching my book to mainstream publishers. While I did feel self-publishing was a vehicle to my ultimate goal of finding a "regular publisher," I never thought the possibility could be so close, so quickly. My advice to every writer is to go for it. Get your work our there in any way you can—including self-publishing and contests. It worked for me, and I'm just a regular person, out there, trying to make it in this very difficult industry!

—Hannah Goodman
Author, *My Sister's Wedding*

Chapter 6

THE PRINT-ON-DEMAND REVOLUTION

If do-it-yourself publishing represents a revolutionary approach to publishing, then print-on-demand (POD) represents a revolutionary approach to printing and distribution.

The advent of POD technology enabled a model of printing and publishing that empowers authors to generate customer demand before printing books. This model, which we call *demand first*, eliminates the need to print books in advance and then warehouse them, because copies are printed only after orders are placed.

With the demand-first system, readers can purchase books by ordering through online retailers, special ordering through retail bookstores, or purchasing copies directly from the author; there is no advance selling to retail stores and no advance printing and warehousing. And, most important, there are few to no returns.

Because POD is affordable and efficient, and breaks the barriers to traditional distribution, it is the method favored at iUniverse.

POD: A BRIEF OVERVIEW

POD is a digital printing process that became commercially viable in the mid-1990s. Using this technology, printers can produce as little as one copy at a time, which can be printed and ready to ship within

The Bookstore-Stocking Distribution-First Printing Model

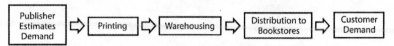

The Demand-First Printing Model

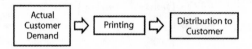

The demand-first model compared to the bookstore-stocking model of printing.

twenty-four hours of an order being placed. The process can be likened to the way your personal computer and printer work together to provide you with paper versions of your stored computer files. At home, when you initiate the print command, your computer sends a digital version of your document to your printer, which produces a hard copy.

POD printing presses work the same way. Book and cover files are kept on computers with enormous file storage capacity, called *servers*. When the press receives an order for a book, the server sends the book and cover files to different printers. The cover printers can print up to eight covers per minute—even if each cover is for a different title. Covers are printed on four-color printers and are then sent to laminating machines. Meanwhile, POD book pages are printed on massive printers using giant rolls of paper. These amazingly efficient POD machines can print five 300-page books per minute.

Benefits of Using POD Technology

No Minimum Print Requirements

As mentioned before, POD printers can economically produce as little as one copy of a book at a time. By contrast, traditional printing, also

An On-Demand Printing Facility.

Photos courtesy of Lightning Source Inc.

called *offset printing*, is economically viable only because of economy of scale.

Although the printing costs per unit are less for traditional printers than for print-on-demand presses, printing a book the old-fashioned way incurs significant expense during what's called the *makeready* stage, in which plates bearing the page images are prepared and the presses are readied for printing. In offset printing, the setup costs, usually called *plant costs*, are the same whether you elect to print five hundred or five thousand books; if you have a large first printing, these costs are spread out, or *amortized*, over a greater number of books, thus lowering the unit cost. In other words, the more books you print, the less each copy costs.

Traditional publishers, then, must print as high a quantity as possible on first runs to keep their cost per book down to a reasonable minimum. In addition, because the cover price of the book is set during the printing stage, setting the per-unit printing cost as low as possible keeps the retail price of the book competitive. On the other hand, traditional publishers know all too well that if they overprint, books will either sit in the warehouse or be returned. It's every traditional publisher's dilemma.

Publishers that use POD, such as iUniverse, sidestep such issues, because the printing technology they use is completely digital. In the digital world, there are no plates, and thus no makeready costs, so each copy costs the same to produce.

For this reason, many traditional publishers now also use POD technology to fulfill orders for *backlist* titles—older books that have low but consistent sales.

No Inventory to Store or Ship

If you choose to fully self-publish and work with a traditional printing press, you will indeed save money by getting thousands of copies printed up front—but, as we pointed out earlier, unless you have a large, secure, moisture-proof garage or another suitable storage area, you'll need to hire a distribution company to store your books safely and fulfill orders. Although a distributor may help you get your book stocked in stores, the expense—along with the likelihood that the books may eventually be returned—make hiring one a costly and risky proposition for inexperienced authors.

The beauty of POD technology is that there's no inventory to store. Your books are printed as they are sold, so you don't have to worry about securing a home for your yet-unsold copies or figuring out an economical way to ship them to buyers.

Extended Life Cycle

Books have a limited shelf life. In traditional publishing, if your title doesn't generate reader demand within a few months, the bookstore will send it back to the publisher, who, in turn, will remainder the book—that is, sell it at a bargain-basement price back to the bookstore. Adding insult to injury, the royalties on such sales, if you receive any at all, are usually vastly reduced depending on the terms of the sale. What's worse is that when copies are gone, the title simply goes out of print.

POD books, on the other hand, do not have predetermined life cycles. In a sense, they never go out of print. No matter how large or small your continuing sales may be, your book can remain in a digital file and available to readers for as long as you choose.

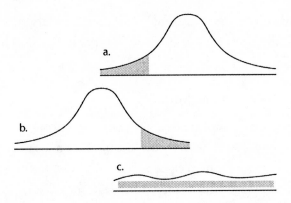

Print-on-demand is the ideal choice for (a) authors who are looking for an alternative way to get started in publishing, (b) authors who wish to keep their books in print at the end of the book life cycle, and (c) authors who are writing for a small but well-defined audience or readership.

Drawbacks to Demand-First Printing

As you've seen, there are pros and cons to every publishing model—and the demand-first alternative is no exception. Here are some of the drawbacks.

Increased Cost per Copy

As mentioned earlier, in offset printing, the more books you print, the less each copy costs, and subsequent printings enjoy even greater savings, because the makeready costs have already been paid. In POD publishing, digitally printed books are generated one at a time, so each copy costs the same amount to print.

Consequently, for books that have a high number of guaranteed sales before printing and require a massive print run, POD may not be as economical as the offset method. (Remember that considerable cost savings arise through traditional printing only if a publisher can average out those costs over several thousand books—and only if those savings are not diluted by the return of unsold copies.)

In time, however, as technology continues to advance, the per-copy cost of POD may come to equal that of offset printing.

Design Limitations

POD publishing is so efficient and economical in large part because it is so standardized. Although POD allows for flexibility in the design and trim size of your book and cover, it is currently designed to produce only paperback and standard hardcover bindings. Unusual trim sizes, special bindings, and interior pop-up and die-cut options are not available.

The quality of digital color printing is very good, however, the per-copy cost of digital printing of book interiors is still nearly cost-prohibitive. Although some POD publishers are willing to pass along these high costs to their authors, iUniverse will only offer interior color printing when the technology evolves enough to make color printing a viable, affordable option for our authors.

Variation in Printing

The quality of POD printing is excellent. Unless you have a trained eye, it is nearly impossible to tell an offset-printed book from one that is printed using POD—as evidenced by the book you are now reading.

The iUniverse books I requested arrived yesterday. I'm embarrassed to say I mistook them for another batch of new books from some big New York City publisher (we get so many review copies) and put them on my "to read" shelf. When I realized what they were, I ran them over to my art director, whose reaction was "Anyone can do this? And it could look like *these*?"

—Stephen George
   Deputy Editor, Features
   Better Homes & Gardens

When books are printed one at a time and different copies are printed days, weeks, or years apart, however, there may be a slight variation from one cover or book interior to the next. Most POD printers allow for a 10 percent variation, which is a negligible difference to most readers.

However, if your book has fine-art illustrations or photographs that you want reprinted with exceptional quality or consistency, or even if you are unwilling to accept slight variations from book to book, then offset printing is your only option. Even then, there are no guarantees—printing is not an exact science.

PRINT-ON-DEMAND AND iUNIVERSE

For authors who are unable to break into the highly exclusive world of traditional publishing and who don't have the time or resources to do it all themselves, POD represents a great alternative.

As you navigate and discuss your publishing options with others, naysayers of supported self-publishing may point out that the retail terms and discount rates that iUniverse and other POD providers offer are not competitive with traditional publishers. However, these critics are missing the point: the demand-first approach works because it doesn't rely on the traditional bookstore-stocking model. Here are the core philosophies behind the retail terms and discounts set by POD publishers and the reasons they work.

The Demand-First Model and Retail Bookstores

The distribution-first model of traditional publishing, with all the cost and risk it entails, is designed with bookstore stocking in mind. That's why traditional publishers carefully consider a book's quality and the author platform before acquiring a title—they know that's what retailers look for when making purchasing decisions.

The demand-first model, however, is designed to bypass traditional gatekeepers and directly reach a wide circle of readers. Therefore, books produced by POD publishers are free from the restraints of the bookstore-stocking model. These books don't require returnability status or deep discounts as purchasing incentives for retailers because advance stocking isn't required; the retailer orders the book only to fulfill a customer order.

That's not to say a retailer won't stock a POD title, however. Most authors believe that a book won't sell unless it is stocked in bookstores. In reality, the situation is quite the reverse: a book won't get stocked unless there is *already* proof that the book will sell. Retailers are businesspeople—they will stock virtually any title that has a steady following and is guaranteed to bring traffic into the store. The POD model gives authors the opportunity to prove that their books will sell through non-traditional channels, providing a guarantee of salability—and that is the best purchasing incentive a retailer could want.

Demand-First Printing and Returns

The practice of selling books to retailers on a fully returnable basis dates back to the Great Depression, when publishers needed to create incentives for retailers to stock books. Today, returns remain a necessary evil for traditional publishers.

Following the traditional distribution-first model, retailers are speculative about stocking titles that do not yet have reader demand, so they require that books be returnable. With the demand-first approach, however, returnablility is not an issue. With the POD model, books are not printed and shipped until they are special-ordered through the retailer or purchased through the bookstore's Web site, removing any risk on the part of the retailer. Think about it: because the retailer has already sold a copy of the book, it won't *need* to make a return to the publisher. Consequently, most POD titles do not need to be returnable.

In addition, when a POD book has steady sales—even if the sales are modest—the retailer is making money. Once you've proven that your book can make money, the retailer will be more apt to stock your title on the shelf—even if the book isn't returnable.

Demand-First Printing and Retail Discounts

Publishers give retailers a discount on a book's cover price. Wholesalers receive an even greater discount and then resell copies of the book, either directly to retailers or to a retail distribution center, which consolidates orders for large retailers and chains. All publishers have standard retail terms and must, by law, give the same discount rate to all retailers within a category.

The greater the discount, the more money the retailer can make; as such, retailers are more likely to stock traditionally published titles that come with higher discounts. If the book doesn't ultimately sell, however, it must be returned—so the discount is beside the point.

Some POD publishers, including iUniverse, must offer lower-than-industry-standard discounts to retailers and wholesalers, mainly because the unit cost of printing and processing these titles is higher. However, as we mentioned before, in retail bookselling, demand and salability trump discount. The only reason retailers are concerned about discount rates on traditional titles is because there's no guarantee those books will sell, which ultimately can affect their bottom lines. Through the demand-first model, you have the chance to offer retailers proof that your book is selling and a guarantee that they will make a profit if they stock it in their stores. Once you do that, discounts don't matter.

Self-Publishing on Your Own and the Demand-First Model

Many authors who self-publish on their own have embraced the demand-first model and are now using POD technology and direct-to-customer distribution methods. However, even with the advantages of POD, these authors must still tackle the complicated, time-consuming, and expensive logistics of taking a book all the way through the editorial, design, and publication processes. So while POD may make full self-publishing somewhat more efficient in terms of time and money, you should still expect the complete do-it-yourself route to amount to a full-time business. If you're not sure you're ready to make that kind of commitment, then read on. iUniverse may be the perfect alternative.

Part 3

GET SUPPORT

Chapter 7

GETTING SUPPORT,
GETTING IT RIGHT

Now that you've considered your publishing options, you can make an educated decision about which alternative provides the best path to your book's publication. If you've decided to forgo the traditional route, you're not on your own: iUniverse can help you achieve your dream of being published professionally, affordably, and as quickly as possible. We offer all of the professional-level services that you'd expect to receive at any traditional publishing house: those in editorial, design and production, and marketing and publicity.

THE EDITORIAL EVALUATION

No matter how small or big an audience you want to reach, the editorial quality of your work matters. If you are asking readers to purchase your book, you've made a promise to them that it contains all the elements expected in a professionally published work. It's up to you to keep that promise.

The Editorial Evaluation is a manuscript checkup that assesses whether it has fulfilled the basic requirements of a professionally published book. An independent, experienced publishing expert reviews the manuscript and offers a professional appraisal of what works and what doesn't. You've worked hard to write your manuscript, but it's even harder to honestly evaluate your own work. An Editorial Evaluation may be your only chance to receive an objective opinion before you make your book available to the public.

The Editorial Evaluation, offered exclusively to iUniverse authors, not only provides a general overview of the editorial readiness of your manuscript to meet expected publishing standards but also educates you on how to write a better manuscript by showing you the factors that are essential in a good book.

In particular, the Editorial Evaluation is an itemized set of criteria that an editorial evaluator uses to assess the editorial quality and content of your book. The questions that evaluators answer differ for fiction, nonfiction, and collections of poetry. These criteria are exactly what agents and editors in traditional publishing consider on some level, however intuitively, so your evaluation is in line with current publishing standards.

Here are some examples of the general questions answered in all Editorial Evaluations:

- Is the category selected to identify the book appropriate for the target audience?

- Is the general structure well-organized, and are the ideas clearly presented?

- Does the last chapter provide an appropriate, meaningful conclusion to the work?

- Does the manuscript contain frequent grammatical, punctuation, or spelling errors?

In addition, the evaluator will answer more specific questions geared toward the kind of book being evaluated: fiction, nonfiction, or poetry. Here is a sampling of questions from each type of Editorial Evaluation.

Nonfiction

- Has the author demonstrated credibility in the subject area?
- Is the material presented in an attractive, consistent, and professional manner?
- Does the content appeal to a wide audience or address a strong niche?
- Is the text supported by appropriate documentation?

Fiction

- Is the basic premise interesting, believable, and unique?
- Do the plot and structure sufficiently hold the reader's interest throughout?
- Are characters believable and introduced for a clear purpose?
- Does the dialogue sound authentic, and is it used effectively throughout?

Poetry

- Do the poem titles appropriately reflect the content of the individual poems?
- Is the metrical scheme appropriate for the subject matter?
- Does the content of the poetry offer multiple levels of meaning (both concrete and abstract)?
- Does the poetry appeal to one or more of the senses?

The Editorial Evaluation not only offers valuable advice on improving your manuscript but also makes you eligible for selection into our prestigious Editor's Choice program, which is a stepping-stone toward admission into the Publisher's Choice and Star programs, described in the next chapter.

Following the advice of an Editorial Evaluation is critical to establishing and maintaining credibility—whether it's with friends, family, colleagues, or book lovers everywhere.

But My Sister's an English Teacher...

It's a myth that a family member, friend, or colleague can be the best editor for your manuscript. In fact, you cannot expect to receive an honest appraisal of your work from those who are close to you—at least without the risk of putting them in an awkward position or harboring resentment once you see their critique of your work. In addition, you probably cannot expect that person to devote the kind of time to your manuscript that a professional editor could. Most important, unless your friends and contacts are professional book editors, their lack of experience in the industry—even if they do have some editing or proofreading skills—is likely to have a negative impact on the quality of your finished manuscript.

Editorial Rx Referrals

When you receive an Editorial Evaluation, the evaluator doesn't just tell you what's amiss; you also get a specific recommendation for the exact level of editorial work your manuscript needs. We call this personalized advice an Editorial Rx Referral.

A Note about the Editorial Rx

If you receive an Editorial Rx Referral for a particular level of editorial work on your manuscript, you have the option to make the changes yourself, hire your own editorial services provider, or employ one of our carefully selected publishing professionals. The choice is yours. The recommendations in the Rx Referral are precisely that—they are suggestions, not requirements. At iUniverse, authors always have the final word.

Because we award Editor's Choice to only the best books, however, iUniverse has to be certain that manuscripts edited by outside providers meet our quality standards. Should you elect to use an alternative service provider or do the work yourself and subsequently want to be considered for the Editor's Choice program, iUniverse will require that you receive a second Editorial Evaluation at a reduced fee.

iUniverse Editorial Services

Behind every good writer is a great editor. Just look at the acknowledgments page in one of your favorite books. The list of people that writers choose to thank for helping them make their books a reality almost always includes an editor.

Anytime I get my work back from an editor, I grind my teeth and reach for the antacids. The fear and anticipation is usually worse than the reality. I read what the editor has said and, frequently, disagree right away. I have to read it a few more times—and take a break—in order to see the wisdom there. It is a scary, messy process but all the more miraculous when your beautiful work shines through better than ever.

—Susan Senator
   Author, *Making Peace with Autism* (Shambhala)
   http://susansenator.com/

Consider the role an editor plays in improving a book. An editor can be a writer's best friend—the kind who gives straightforward advice, but can deliver it in a way that is tactful. An editor provides an objective pair of eyes to spot flaws that the author, who is simply too personally involved in the work, cannot see. A good editor can turn your ordinary sentences into extraordinary prose without compromising the essence of your voice or the intent of your message.

Unfortunately, finding an experienced professional editor can be a catch-22, especially for first-time authors. Traditional publishing houses won't assign an editor to you until they've accepted your book, but they won't accept your book if it needs editorial work. iUniverse has the solution: we offer editorial services from experienced freelance editors—often the same editors used by traditional publishers—for fees that are at or below industry rates.

---

iUniverse Editorial Services

If necessary, your editorial evaluator will provide you with an Rx Referral to an appropriate editorial specialist, ranging from a *copyeditor* to a *book doctor*, who can help improve your manuscript by giving it the kind of attention you'd receive from editors at a traditional publishing house. In fact, our editors come from the same pool of freelance service providers that major publishing companies use.

The editorial services we offer are available to iUniverse authors only. For details about eligibility, fees, and the time required for each service, go to iUniverse.com.

---

iUniverse Editorial Services fall under three primary levels: core services, advanced services, and post-production services.

Core Editorial Services

Core editing services focus on improving the nuts and bolts of a book: grammar, mechanics, structure, and if applicable, continuity.

Copyediting

An experienced copyeditor will carefully check your manuscript, correcting errors in spelling, grammar, punctuation, and syntax. In addition, they will verify cross-references and impose industry-standard style.

Line Editing

When heavier editing is required, a line editor will not only check the manuscript line by line for moderate errors in spelling, grammar, and punctuation, but also make suggestions regarding sentence structure and word choice. A line editor may also recommend light structural changes to improve the overall readability of the work.

Content Editing

In addition to performing the functions of a line edit, a content editor will work to ensure the general accuracy and consistency of content and focus on more extensive restructuring of sentences. For fiction titles, the editor will focus on maintaining consistency of details in the plot, characters, and setting. For nonfiction titles, the editor will monitor consistency of information and ideas.

I would like to express my deep appreciation to the content editor.

It may not have been obvious to the editor, but my manuscript had been read by three other editors and six other readers. Of course, these were friends and colleagues, none of whom read it in as much detail as this editor.

I was amazed at the detailed comments the content editor made. The changes helped strengthen characterization and eliminate inconsistencies in the plot. Imposing a consistent style throughout the book drastically reduced distractions for the reader.

What the content edit has done is to eliminate the unintended barriers for the reader and make the story shine.

—David Crouse
Author, *War by Other Means*

Advanced Editorial Services

For books that need attention to big-picture issues—those that go beyond detail work in grammar, spelling, and punctuation—iUniverse offers the following services.

Developmental Editing

A developmental editor provides a substantive, in-depth analysis of the editorial work needed on a manuscript, giving advice on overall editorial issues at the paragraph, chapter, and book levels. At traditional publishing houses, this is generally the work performed by the in-house editor who acquired the book.

At iUniverse, the developmental editor provides a sample edit to the author and awaits feedback before proceeding. Once the author reviews and approves the sample, the editor continues making recommendations throughout the remainder of the manuscript. Developmental editors do not make the changes; they tell the author what and how a manuscript may be improved.

For a fiction manuscript, the developmental editor analyzes the readership and genre to determine whether the content is appropriate and makes recommendations with regard to such essential elements as plot, pacing, characterization, point of view, and dialogue. For nonfiction titles, the editor analyzes the readership, purpose, and possible uses of the work while determining whether the content is complete and appropriate; the concepts are developed adequately; the material is well organized; and the illustrations, tables, lists, and other graphic elements are clear, appealing, and used effectively.

Upon completion of a Developmental Editing service, iUniverse returns the manuscript to the author along with an hourly estimate for the optional Book Doctor service (described in the next section).

After the advice suggested by the developmental editor has been implemented, either by the author or by a book doctor, the manuscript undergoes a content edit—one of our core services—at no extra cost.

Should You Invest in Advanced Editorial Services?

When deciding whether to purchase an editorial service, consider the goals for your book. For example, if you wrote the book for a close circle of friends and relatives, investing time and money in a developmental edit and the services of a book doctor may or may not be warranted. If you come from a family of English teachers, however, an editorial service of some type might indeed be a good idea—or you'll likely hear about that misplaced modifier at every family gathering for years to come! If you plan to sell a book to industry colleagues or to the general public, professional editing is essential.

Book Doctoring

Only books that have undergone an iUniverse Developmental Edit are eligible for the Book Doctor service, because a book doctor implements the advice recommended by the developmental editor. The book doctor provides a sample edit to the author and awaits feedback before proceeding. Upon completion of the Book Doctor service, and after author approval of the final draft, the manuscript undergoes a Content Editing service at no extra cost.

Remember that following the advice of a professional editor takes time and careful consideration and that developmental editing, in particular, often requires the author to rewrite or reorganize the manuscript to enhance existing material. Therefore, the best choice for authors who don't have the time or ability to make the big-picture changes recommended by a developmental editor may be to hire a book doctor.

Ghostwriting

In some cases, an author may need to consider hiring a ghostwriter—a professional writer with general knowledge of a particular subject—to work on a manuscript. Using a first draft of the manuscript or other rough materials provided by the author, such as notes, interview transcripts, and reports, the ghostwriter writes the book in consultation with the author. The cost of the Ghostwriting service is determined when the ghostwriter examines the materials provided by the author and creates a writing sample, delivery schedule, and price estimate for the author's approval.

Researching

Family memoirs and novels, or nonfiction titles requiring precise and accurate details (e.g., historical, technological, military) may benefit from the assistance of researchers knowledgeable in specific subject areas. The Researcher service includes informational researchers who gather data, statistics, and other information, as well as photo researchers and graphic artists. Authors interested in this service must complete a questionnaire to help us determine their specific needs and develop a per-hour cost estimate.

Developmental Editing and Book Doctor Services

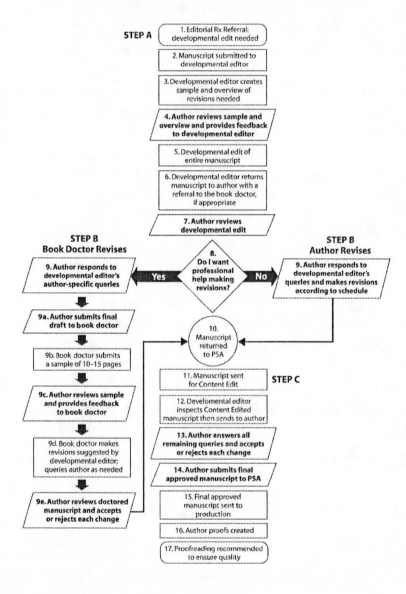

Post-Production Editorial Services

The quest for editorial quality shouldn't end when your manuscript has gone to production. Post-production quality checks are equally important in creating a positive first impression of your book. iUniverse makes the following services available:

Proofreading

Although the final version of your manuscript will be professionally designed and typeset, mistakes can sometimes occur during the conversion of your manuscript into a formatted book. In addition, even careful authors and exacting editors miss a few errors, so it's a good idea to have a professional proofreader examine the book a final time before it goes to print. Proofreaders look for typographical and mechanical errors such as misspellings, missing words, and incorrect cross-references. They also check margins, word breaks, headings, and letter and word spacing to ensure that the final product is readable and consistent, and meets predetermined specifications. A character-by-character proofread of your book can save you from embarrassment and from costly corrections after publication.

Indexing

An index compiled by a professional indexer can maximize the usability of a nonfiction title. Although indexes can also be automatically generated by computers, a computer-generated list of key words may not be sufficient for selling your book in certain markets; many library distributors, for example, will not accept a book unless it contains a custom-made index. In addition, computer-generated indexes that list a page number for a key term every time it occurs in the book are not very useful; they are excessively long and have no logical organization other than alphabetization.

A professional indexer analyzes your book, anticipates line items your reader will most likely want to find, and lists them in an intuitive, accessible manner. Mainstream publishers opt to use indexes custom-made by a professional because they are more useful and accessible to the reader. Simply put, people read books; computers don't.

Before handcrafting your one-of-a-kind index, our professional indexer considers the following four elements that make your book unique:

- Focus

- Purpose

- Audience

- Organization

The end result is an industry-standard, two-level index, fully copy-edited for quality assurance.

Copywriting (Cover Copy Polish)

When you're shopping in a grocery store, how do you decide which product to buy? Often, whether you're aware of it or not, the message or call-to-action on the packaging makes the difference between your selecting one brand and your selecting another. Think of your cover copy as the packaging that will entice a reader to purchase your book. The average book superstore stocks more than 100,000 titles, most of which are displayed spine-out. If a browser happens to pull one off the shelf for a better look, he'll spend about four seconds gazing at the front cover before flipping the book over to read the copy on the back. At that point, you've got about seven seconds to make the sale, so whatever you say needs to speak to him directly.

The title, subtitle, and any other copy that appears on the front of the book are the most important elements of your book's cover. In addition, although the back cover probably won't be the first thing prospective readers notice about your book, in all likelihood, it will be the first part they actually read, and readers typically decide whether to buy a book based on what its back cover has to say. The title and front cover attract a buyer's attention; the back cover copy clinches the sale.

iUniverse offers the services of professional copywriters to polish the invaluable copy that appears on your covers—both front and back. Our marketing professionals know that creating the right title and cover content for your book is critical to its success, so they work to ensure that your title is focused and inviting and that the back cover copy propels a potential buyer to purchase your book. In addition, a copywriter works with you to create an author bio that reflects your strengths, and—if you've chosen to get your book in a hardcover edition—the copywriter rewrites the copy for the inside flaps. They also create a marketing keynote, which is a concise sales and marketing handle that you can use to pitch your work to booksellers, the media, and ultimately, the reading public.

iUNIVERSE DESIGN SERVICES

Package design is a $50 billion business in America. In fact, more money is spent on designing the packages for shampoo, cereal, household cleaners, and other consumer goods than on manufacturing the actual products. Consumers base their buying decisions for a whole host of products more on the packaging than on what's inside—and books are no different. We've discussed the two key questions that professionals in the book business always ask: is it good and will it sell? In today's visually oriented world, a third question is as essential: does it *look* good?

You Do Judge a Book by Its Cover

The old saying "You can't judge a book by its cover" may be sage advice when it comes to making first impressions of people, but ironically, it doesn't apply to the bookselling business. Agents, booksellers, reviewers, and a host of other industry professionals, as well as average consumers, do judge books by their covers, forming quick and lasting first impressions based on little more than appearance.

Original Submitted Back Cover Copy
Cryptid, by Eric Penz

FICTION

Lewis and Clark's story is one we all know well. It is at the heart of American lore, and is perhaps one of the greatest legends in human history. But the story told in textbooks and classrooms is not the whole story. For their true mission and what they actually discovered on the shores of the Pacific have been close guarded secrets of the government since Thomas Jefferson handpicked Lewis to lead the Corps. of Discovery.

Even today, two hundred years later, the truth is being suppressed. And not only by the government. Each of us has been deceived by the most invisible of conspiracies, for the conspiracy lies within our own minds, blinding us to a truth that is contrary to everything we believe about our unique status among the inhabitants of earth. The truth is we are not alone. There is other intelligent life on earth.

Two centuries in the making, *Cryptid* is the final chapter to Lewis and Clark's story. And as with any good story the best secrets have been kept until the end.

Photo credit: Wayne Waldroup

Eric Penz is a partner in an insurance and financial services agency in Redmond, WA. He earned his bachelors of science degree in environmental biology from Eastern Washington University in 1995. His postgraduate work was done at the University of Washington where he completed a two-year literary program in commercial fiction. In-between managing his clients' portfolios and writing, he spends his spare time as an amateur adventure athlete.

He and his wife and their two boys make their home in Issaquah, WA. Visit the author's website at www.ericpenz.com, or for more information on Gigantopithecus and the latest Sasquatch sightings visit www.cryptid.com.

ISBN 0-595-35974-4

51895

9 780595 359745

www.iuniverse.com

$18.95U.S.

iUniverse®
Editor's Choice

After Cover Copy Polish
Cryptid, by Eric Penz

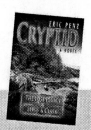

FICTION

The line between history and legend can be deceptively thin—too thin perhaps to maintain the claim that one is exclusively fact and one fiction. Such may be the case with the history of Lewis and Clark. For the fact is that two hundred years after they were handpicked by Thomas Jefferson to lead an extraordinary expedition to the Pacific Coast legends still persist regarding unexplained gaps in the explorers' field journals.

Call it legend, call it history, *Cryptid* tells the riveting story of conspiracy theorists who have new evidence of a centuries-old cover-up. When a cryptozoologist, a paleontologist, and a Jefferson descendant begin connecting the dots, they threaten to do more than unveil the well-guarded scientific discovery that lies at the heart of the ancient secret; they threaten to rewrite American history. That is if they can survive a conspiracy that dates back to the Founding Fathers—the very same that haunted Lewis to his grave. It may be that one of our nation's first secrets is still being kept.

Cryptid illustrates how the human act of seeking the truth can be the very element that destroys it. Two centuries in the making, *Cryptid* is the final chapter of the Lewis and Clark story. As with any good tale, the best secrets have been kept until the end.

Photo credit: Wayne Waldroup

Eric Penz is a partner in an insurance and financial services agency. Between managing his clients' portfolios and writing, he spends his spare time as an amateur adventure athlete. He and his wife and their two boys make their home in Issaquah, Washington.

ISBN 0-595-35974-4

5 1895

9 780595 359745

$18.95 U.S.

www.iuniverse.com

Many readers who don't know the first thing about you or your writing will pick up your book to consider whether it's worth reading—but only if something catches their eye. Once they notice it and get it into their hands, many consumers will decide whether to buy your book based solely on the way it looks and feels.

Custom-Designed Book Covers

All books published by iUniverse, except for those that go through our no-frills package, receive customized full-color covers. If you elect our reduced-rate package, you'll get to choose your cover design from a variety of attractive and eye-catching cover templates. For all other publishing packages, our design team will work with you—incorporating your photos, graphics, sketches, and ideas—to create a custom-designed book cover that is as unique to your work as it is beautifully representative of your subject matter.

In all cases, your front cover will include your book's title, subtitle, your name or pseudonym, and other marketing copy or advance quotes, if suitable. We'll also put together an eye-catching back cover, using the author bio and back cover copy you provide. If space allows, we can also incorporate an author photo and endorsements.

The iUniverse Design Concept Evaluation

The Design Concept Evaluation, available only through the Premier Plus package (detailed in Chapter 9), provides authors with the services of a design evaluator who has extensive experience in traditional book publishing. Although we do custom covers for nearly all titles, the Design Concept Evaluation takes the process one step further. In the same way that an experienced editor assesses the overall quality of a manuscript in the iUniverse Editorial Evaluation (also included in the Premier Plus package), the design evaluator makes sure that your cover idea is both suitable for the subject and category of your book, and meets industry retail standards.

Here's how it works:

1. Tell us your cover design idea during the online submission process. Once your manuscript reaches the Design Concept Evaluation stage, we'll ask you for more specific information, which we will use to guide our professional design team in creating a cover that best suits your book.

2. A design evaluator will review your ideas and any art you may have provided to ensure that your vision for your cover translates clearly into precise instructions to the designer, is appropriate for the target audience, and meets book-industry standards. In some cases, the evaluator may recommend a more commercially viable concept. Once the concept is finalized, an iUniverse designer will create an attractive and appropriate cover for your book under the direct supervision of our experienced art director.

3. Once the cover has been developed, you will have the chance to review the final design and to accept or reject it. The design evaluator and our expert design team are available to give you helpful guidance, but at iUniverse you have the final word.

My thanks to the design department at iUniverse—I love the cover! I let your e-mail sit in my inbox for two hours while I gathered my nerve to open it. It came out better than I could hope for. You guys are the pros and you brought my ideas to life in a graphic yet simple way. And I have to say that based on the experience I am having with regard to speed and quality, your company will quickly be setting a new standard and will be a shining light and example of how the industry should work.

—Eric Penz
   Author, *Cryptid*

Book Formatting

All manuscripts submitted to iUniverse are formatted as trade paperbacks and printed on high-quality, acid-free, book-grade opaque paper stock in black-and-white or grayscale halftones. Paperback covers are printed on a bright white cover stock in full color with a professional gloss coating. The size of your final book depends on your personal preferences and on the publishing package you purchase.

Manuscripts submitted under all but the basic-level publishing packages are automatically produced in eBook format. An eBook is an electronic version of a book that readers can download and read on a computer or on a handheld PDA. For your protection, eBooks cannot be transferred, copied, or printed.

Authors may choose the hardcover option as an add-on to all but the basic package. Hardcover books feature a durable cloth binding, an embossed spine, and a full-color dust jacket.

MARKETING AND PUBLICITY SERVICES

If you want your book to sell, it's not enough to publish it and hope for the best. After all, no one can purchase your work if they don't know it exists. Your book's success and the resulting revenue strongly depend on the quality of your marketing and publicity efforts. Moreover, a good marketing plan is a big step toward positively addressing the question asked by publishing professionals: will it sell?

iUniverse is continually forming alliances to offer our authors new and effective ways to market. The marketing and publicity services available only to iUniverse authors can serve as your launchpad to a unique and dynamic marketing platform.

The Marketing Toolkit

The Marketing Toolkit features a set of templates prepared by professional designers that you can use to create your own press releases, sell sheet, events signs, postcards, bookmarks, business cards, posters, and Web site banner ads, and includes guidelines for effectively using each of these promotional tools to generate demand for your book.

I want to commend iUniverse on its fantastic Marketing Toolkit. I've been in marketing and public relations for years, and this is one of the best guides I've encountered. The information is cutting-edge, and it's easy to read and follow. Great job!

—Linda Brown Holt
    Author, *Viewing Meister Eckhart through the Bhagavad Gita*

The Marketing Success Workbook

This comprehensive guide for developing a marketing strategy tailored to your book provides a simple-to-follow, three-step approach that will help you pinpoint your target audience and identify your unique selling skills. You'll then be able to determine the promotional tactics most suited to your talents and preferences, and pull them all together into a coordinated and well-timed marketing plan.

The Publicity Success Kit

If you're ready to start publicizing your book, but you're not sure how to begin, consider the Publicity Success Kit. This comprehensive package, available only to Editor's Choice authors, contains the instructions, advice, and contacts you will need to systematically and effectively publicize your work, as well as detailed media contact information—including the names of individual media contacts, their phone and fax numbers, and their e-mail and mailing addresses.

Specifically, the Publicity Success Kit includes

- Instructions on how to pitch your book to the media
- Tips for writing effective cover letters and press releases

- Sample interview questions
- Interview dos and don'ts
- Tips on how to build your book publicity campaign

Using the materials in the Publicity Success Kit, you can reach your market through the same outlets that professional publicists use:

- Radio, television, magazine, newspaper, Internet media, and wire services
- Awards and contests
- Community newsletters, forums, and bulletin boards

Each Publicity Success Kit contains media contact information for one state of your choice. Media contacts for additional states are available for an extra fee. In addition, if your book is a mystery, self-help, or new age title, you may request additional media contacts for your specific genre.

The Personal Publicist

Hiring a personal publicist from iUniverse takes the guesswork out of the all-important process of promoting your book.

From the magazine reviews to local media to national media, my iUniverse publicist's dedication and professional attitude throughout my publicity campaign is the reason for my book's success. I received e-mails early in the morning and late at night, indicative of someone who not only works diligently to succeed but also cares that others read my book. I sincerely felt my publicist had as much pride in my book and accomplishment as I did.

—Dean Gualco
  Author, *The Meaning of Life*

Every Editor's Choice author has the option of hiring a book publicist, who not only writes your press materials but also explores ways to tie your book to current news, so that you have a better-than-average chance of making an impact in the media. Your publicist will aggressively seek out all of the Web sites, printed publications, and broadcast media that reach your intended audience to help you promote your book and build sales. After e-mailing and faxing your press releases to selected media, your personal publicist will follow up with each contact to pitch your book, arrange interviews, and confirm articles and reviews.

---

iUniverse provided me with an attentive, open-minded publicist who worked closely with me, and months later I'm still seeing results.

—R. J. Revaitis
Author, *Park Avenue Rich*

Why Hire a Book Publicist?

If you want to build readership and generate sales for your book, you'll need to get the word out. Publicity is the most cost-effective form of promotion, and here's the proof:

- Compared to paid advertisements, book publicity can be an inexpensive means of reaching your target audience and selling your book. Consider, for example, that a quarter-page advertisement in *USA Today* could set you back about $10,000. If your publicity campaign generates even one article in a national newspaper or magazine, then your promotional effort has more than paid for itself.

- Book publicity carries greater credibility among reading audiences than does paid advertising. Your readers will know that you didn't pay to be interviewed by that talk show host or to be mentioned in that feature article or that positive review of your book in last Sunday's newspaper. If you didn't pay for the message, then your audience can trust it to be unbiased and accurate.

Printed Bookselling Materials

The Printed Bookselling Materials package consists of full-color post-cards, bookmarks, and business cards featuring your book. You'll find a multitude of ways to use these handy and colorful giveaways—tuck them inside your press kit, hand them out at book fairs, and give them to fans at book signings. Each package includes all three sales aids (postcards, bookmarks, and business cards), and is available in quantities of 100, 300, or 400 of each.

Co-op Advertising

Stop wishing you could advertise your book to a national audience and make it happen. iUniverse brings authors together by genre to promote their books directly to their target audience. By pooling resources for a single ad, several authors can affordably advertise their books in widely circulated publications that would otherwise be out of reach. iUniverse coordinates, schedules, and designs each ad on behalf of participating authors.

The Kirkus Discoveries Book Review

Getting your book reviewed is perhaps one of the most challenging yet essential tasks for any newly published author. A positive book review from a well-respected publication can lend a great deal of credibility to a new title that is attempting to find its niche within the marketplace. But with nearly 200,000 titles published each year, the competition for reviews is fierce.

iUniverse has teamed with Kirkus Discoveries to streamline the review process for our authors. The resulting service gives you the opportunity to have your title reviewed by *Kirkus Reviews*, one of the most prominent and respected book review publications in the publishing industry.

Kirkus Discoveries is a paid review service from the editors of *Kirkus Reviews* that gives self-published authors the chance to be noticed in today's competitive marketplace. Kirkus employs experienced book reviewers who have expertise in various fields. All reviews are posted on the Discoveries Web site and are eligible for inclusion in the Kirkus Discoveries monthly eNewsletter, which highlights the best submissions to the program at no extra cost. The eNewsletter goes to a targeted base of subscribers, many of whom are shopping for the print and film rights to books.

Press Materials

Informative and professional-looking press materials are among the most important elements of any marketing campaign. Using information you provide, our publicity staff creates a basic publicity package for your book, including a unique selling point or hook, a cover-letter template, and a press release.

Clipping Service

When you subscribe to our clipping service, iUniverse will monitor more than 18,000 publications nationwide for your name and the title of your book so that you'll know every time you and your book are mentioned. This is an easy and economical way to gauge the effectiveness of your publicity campaign.

Google Book Search

If you choose, iUniverse will enter your book into the Google Book Search Partner Program, a specialized search on Google.com that enables users to search the full text of books to find titles of interest, view a small portion of the book, and then find online bookstores where they may purchase them. See Chapter 12 for ways that this service can help you with your online marketing.

LEVELING THE PLAYING FIELD

For any dedicated author who comes to iUniverse for supported self-publishing services, the bottom line is this: work hard not only to make your book the best it can be, but also to build a following of readers. If you do, iUniverse will give you what you need to broaden your book's quality and commercial appeal.

Chapter 8

RECOGNIZING QUALITY, ACCELERATING SUCCESS

As you've learned in many parts of this book, quality matters in both the content of your work and the look of the cover. You've also discovered that iUniverse is committed to helping you make your book the best it can be—inside and out. We make an effort to recognize the best books with special programs that can help accelerate their authors' success.

The iUniverse Editor's Choice designation is the first acknowledgment that your book positively answers that all-important question that publishing professionals and readers ask about each and every book: is it good?

EDITOR'S CHOICE

With the huge number of titles available for purchase today, along with high cover prices, readers often seek help in choosing from the glut of books in the marketplace. They ask friends for recommendations, read consumer-generated and professional reviews, and look for titles that have earned awards or that carry some cachet by virtue of an author's credentials or industry recognition. iUniverse titles that receive a positive Editorial Evaluation, or are satisfactorily revised according to the Editorial Evaluation's recommendations, qualify for consideration as an Editor's Choice title. The iUniverse Editor's Choice designation is our way of saying, quite simply: this book is good.

The Benefits of Editor's Choice

The following benefits are available only to authors whose books receive the Editor's Choice designation:

- *The Editor's Choice Icon*: Titles accepted into the Editor's Choice program carry the Editor's Choice icon on their back covers. In addition, Editor's Choice books are featured in a separate designated section of the iUniverse online bookstore.

- *Awards Submissions*: Many contests and awards for published material require that the publisher, rather than the author, submit a book for consideration. Editor's Choice authors are invited to send the appropriate entry forms to our publicity staff, who then forward the materials to the respective judging committees.

- *The Publicity Success Kit*: The Publicity Success Kit helps build the kind of media buzz for your book that traditional book publicists create on behalf of their clients. This comprehensive kit contains detailed media contact information for your geographical region and gives you tips on how to pitch your book and build an effective publicity campaign.

- *A Personal Publicist*: If you'd rather not handle publicity on your own, you can hire an iUniverse book publicist. Our publicists create press materials tailored to your title, pitch your book to the media, arrange interviews, and confirm reviews.

PUBLISHER'S CHOICE

iUniverse represents a model of publishing and distribution that enables authors to eliminate the middlemen and market books directly to their readers. However, we also understand that many authors dream of seeing their books on display at the local bookstore. That's why iUniverse has partnered with the largest retail chain, Barnes & Noble, to offer a reward that is unparalleled in nontraditional publishing—the opportunity for your book to be featured on the new releases table in your local Barnes & Noble store. This reward is only available to authors who receive the iUniverse Publisher's Choice designation.

Qualifications for Publisher's Choice

Books become eligible for Publisher's Choice when they meet these requirements:

- The iUniverse Editor's Choice designation.

- A book cover that meets industry standards established by a positive iUniverse Design Concept Evaluation (available only with the Premier Plus package).

The iUniverse Publisher's Choice designation is an example of our dedication to identify, support, and celebrate those titles that display potential for greater commercial success. Titles in our top publishing package, Premier Plus, which you'll learn about in the next chapter, receive professional editorial and design evaluations; those titles that meet industry standards in the evaluations are awarded Publisher's Choice.

The Benefits of Publisher's Choice

- Publisher's Choice titles become eligible for display on the New Paperback Releases table in one Barnes & Noble store for at least eight weeks.

- Authors receive the support they need to develop a customized marketing plan. This support includes marketing tips and ideas, a marketing plan template, a title information sheet template, and the opportunity to communicate one-on-one with an iUniverse marketing associate.

- After authors develop their marketing plan and title information sheet, iUniverse submits these documents to a national buyer at Barnes & Noble. This buyer will determine at what location to stock the books as well as the number of books to purchase for the stocking period.

- After a book has been in the store for eight weeks, Barnes & Noble will evaluate how well the book sold during its stocking period. If the book generated significant demand, the store may continue to stock the title in the appropriate section.

READER'S CHOICE

Qualifications for Reader's Choice

Books become eligible for Reader's Choice when they meet these qualifications:

- The iUniverse Editor's Choice designation.

- Sales of 250 copies or more. Half of the 250 copies must have been sold through retail channels.

The Reader's Choice designation goes beyond recognizing quality in a book's editorial and design elements to distinguishing an author's proven ability to sell books. Meeting the required number of sales to attain Reader's Choice indicates that a receptive market exists for your book and proves that your personal marketing efforts are working.

The Benefits of Reader's Choice

Authors who earn the Reader's Choice designation are eligible for the following benefits:

- *Publicity Teleseminars*: By participating in these monthly interactive telephone seminars with a book publicity specialist and other authors, you can receive personal advice on promoting your book from field experts.

- *The Reader's Choice Newsletter*: This monthly newsletter contains exclusive tips on publicity opportunities and special advice on sales. It provides information about the publishing industry and innovative methods for successfully marketing your book.

- *The Reader's Choice Icon*: In the iUniverse online bookstore, Reader's Choice books are identified with the designation's exclusive icon next to their titles' listings and are featured in a separate section of the site.

THE STAR PROGRAM

Qualifications for the Star Program

Each author whose book has met the following qualifications will receive an invitation to apply for the Star designation:

- The iUniverse Editor's Choice and Reader's Choice designations.

- Sales of 500 or more copies, at least 250 of which have been sold through retail channels, including both online and brick-and-mortar bookstores.

The Star Program gives iUniverse the opportunity to identify, celebrate, and support titles that display a particularly high level of editorial excellence as well as those that have shown promising sales. This program, which is unique among publishing service providers, helps our most successful authors level the playing field in today's highly competitive marketplace.

Star Program Benefits

The Star Program provides the following benefits:

- A professional cover reassessment, including revision of the cover copy and author bio, a new ISBN, and the addition of the Star imprint logo. iUniverse will also create a new front cover, if necessary.

- An invitation to participate in a free personal consultation with iUniverse editorial, marketing, and publicity professionals.

- A professional editorial polish and marketing support, if warranted, at iUniverse expense.

In addition, every Star title is

- Featured on the iUniverse Web site, along with an author bio.

- Eligible to receive industry-standard discounts and returnability status for book retailers.

- Presented to buyers at Barnes & Noble to be considered for regional or national in-store placement.

- Submitted for a Kirkus Discoveries review.

- Considered for possible submission to foreign publishers for translation rights, if suitable.

Qualifying for the Star Program

iUniverse uses the same criterion when considering your book as a candidate for the Star Program that traditional-industry professionals use during the acquisitions process, and we ask the same questions that continually echo throughout this book: is it good and will it sell?

Editorial Quality

To qualify for the Star Program, books must have received our Editor's Choice designation, which recognizes commercial-quality book content. However, we provide additional editorial services, if necessary, for books that have been accepted into the Star Program—to make them even better.

Early Commercial Success

In today's competitive publishing environment, editorial quality is only the first step toward success. Not only must authors be good writers; they must be energetic marketers as well. Authors often first reach their target audiences through nontraditional bookselling channels, such as specialty stores and online retailers, and through direct sales to audiences who attend speaking engagements or niche events. In effect, they take advantage of these nontraditional methods to help them hone their skills and test-market their book.

To qualify for Star status, iUniverse authors must prove they can develop an enthusiastic following by selling an above-average number of their books through retail channels. Just as sales of traditionally published titles demonstrate marketability, sales of self-published books in retail outlets prove that an author has targeted a book-buying audience and that he knows how to reach that audience using methods beyond direct sales.

Applying for the Star Program

Once you've achieved the necessary editorial and commercial milestones, iUniverse will extend you a formal invitation to apply for the Star Program. Each month, the iUniverse Star Review Board meets to review completed applications and discuss the eligibility of selected titles for the program. The Board considers these questions, among others:

- Does the book have an innovative, fresh, and unique style? Is the author familiar with competitive titles and able to articulate why her book has its own special appeal that distinguishes it from similar titles?

- Is the book in a genre that sells well?

- Does the author demonstrate an understanding of the book's target audience and effective ways to reach that audience? How does the author's understanding translate into current, lifetime, and potential sales?

- Is the author willing and able to continue to generate customer demand for the title? What level of investment is required to support that effort?

- Most important, will the book benefit from the features offered as part of the Star Program?

At the conclusion of their discussion of eligible titles each month, the Star Review Board notifies the authors who have been accepted into this prestigious program.

What's Next: After the Star Program

Once a Star author reaches the full potential of the program and attains an exceptional level of success, iUniverse may formally present the Star title to traditional industry players such as publishers, agents, and scouts. Of course, the author always has the final decision regarding whether to accept a traditional publishing contract, to sign with an agent—or to continue in the Star Program. As the following success stories demonstrate, many authors who made the leap from iUniverse to traditional publishing are reaping significant benefits as a result.

WHAT AUTHORS HAVE TO SAY

I planned a nationally-publicized 1,200-mile walk but couldn't find a publisher for my story. I published with iUniverse and within ninety days, *Big & Tall Chronicles* was available for sale. As I trekked from Florida to Massachusetts, I sold more and more books and quickly earned Star status for my efforts. One special day, iUniverse called to tell me that *Big & Tall Chronicles* would be available for sale regionally in Barnes & Noble. With the help of iUniverse, I've been able to motivate thousands of other overweight Americans to change their lives for the better.

—Gary Marino
   Author, *Big & Tall Chronicles*

When I originally wrote *Life Lessons for My Black Girls* in 2000, I was told by traditional publishers that there wasn't a market for inspirational nonfiction for African American girls. So I decided to take control of my publishing future and turned to iUniverse to help me self-publish my book. It was a decision that changed my life. I sold over 15,000 copies and became one of the first iUniverse Star authors to have a book stocked in Barnes & Noble. In 2005, Hyperion signed me to a six-figure, two-book deal and renamed the book *Life Lessons for My Sisters*. None of it would have been possible without iUniverse.

—Natasha Munson
   Author, *Life Lessons for My Sisters*

After I retired from a rewarding career as a professor and practicing psychologist, I decided to focus on writing. I published my book, *The Anger Habit*, through iUniverse and was selected for the Star Program based on the early sales success of the book. Barnes & Noble agreed to stock my title and the word continued to spread—all the way to Sourcebooks, a traditional publisher that has now republished *The Anger Habit* and signed me to a three-book deal with an advance. With the help of iUniverse, I've embarked on a *third* successful career.

—Carl Semmelroth
   Author, *The Anger Habit*

Part 4

GET PUBLISHED

Chapter 9

CHOOSING A PUBLISHING PACKAGE
THAT'S RIGHT FOR YOU

You've written a book, established your goals, determined what services you need to make your book the best it can be, and examined the realities of the marketplace—now you can leave the publishing details to us.

iUniverse publishing packages provide unique combinations of editorial, design, marketing, and other services, allowing you to choose the package that best suits your needs. When a quick turnaround is essential, choose the package that will get your book to market in thirty days or fewer. To ensure that your manuscript is well organized and error-free, choose one of the packages that provides you with a thorough Editorial Evaluation. In order to maximize your publicity and marketing efforts, go with a package that includes practical tools such as our Marketing Success Workbook and Marketing Toolkit. And, of course, please call us if you're not sure and need help to find the package that will put you on the appropriate path to achieving your goals.

MAKE PUBLISHING EASIER—CHOOSE A PACKAGE

iUniverse offers five publishing packages, allowing you to choose the one that is the best fit for your schedule, your budget, and your goals.

Regardless of which package you choose, you can expect to receive the following benefits:

- **Quicker-than-average turnaround.** Traditional publishers typically take a year or more to bring a book to market. At iUniverse, we can turn your manuscript into a finished book in as few as thirty days.

- **One-on-one author support.** The staff at iUniverse knows that the publishing process can be somewhat overwhelming, especially for first-time authors, so we're prepared to walk you through every step. At the same time, we never forget that we are helping you with *your* book and that you have the final say on matters regarding its editing, design, and marketing.

- **Great discounts.** We know you'll need books on hand to give as gifts and to use for promotional purposes, so we offer some of the best author discounts in the business—but we never impose a minimum quantity of books you must order. All iUniverse authors may purchase copies of their own titles for between 20 and 30 percent below the listed retail price. Discounts for large-volume orders (100 copies or more) range from 45 to 65 percent off the list price. If you arrange for a special event, such as a book signing, we'll make books available at reduced rates and ship them directly to the retailer or the venue hosting your event.

- **Nonexclusive contracts.** iUniverse maintains a nonexclusive policy with regard to author contracts with no term of license, which means you can cancel the contract at any time. This is especially good news for books that are successful in the marketplace. If your book attracts the attention of a traditional publisher who offers to take over the publication of your work, or if you choose to fully self-publish at any time, all you have to do is notify us.

- **Inclusion in the iUniverse online bookstore.** As an iUniverse author, your book automatically receives a listing on our Web site and is available for purchase through the iUniverse online bookstore.

- **ISBN assignment.** iUniverse assigns every title an ISBN (International Standard Book Number)—a machine-readable thirteen-digit number that uniquely identifies your book for retailers and libraries.

In addition, you will be eligible for a wide range of features and services (described in Chapter 7), that are either included or available as options in the Select, Premier, and Premier Plus packages. These services include:

- **Professional editorial services.** iUniverse offers the same array of editorial services—from the same pool of professional freelancers—that you'd get from a traditional publisher. Starting with the cornerstone of our editorial services line-up, the iUniverse Editorial Evaluation, we are dedicated to helping you make your book the best it can be, and we offer every type of editing available—from basic copyediting to advanced developmental editing and even ghostwriting.

- **Industry-standard cover design.** In addition to the custom cover we create for each title, our new Design Concept Evaluation, offered in our Premier Plus package, ensures that the all-important cover of your book not only represents your vision but is also suitable for the competitive marketplace.

- **Publicity and marketing support.** Once your book is published, our marketing and publicity services help you create a unique and dynamic platform from which to effectively promote and sell your book—from a Marketing Toolkit that will help you create custom promotional materials to our clipping service, which will keep track of your successes in the media. For titles that receive the iUniverse Editor's Choice distinction, there are other comprehensive services and tools available, including the option to hire a personal publicist who will aggressively seek outlets to get your book noticed.

- **Worldwide distribution.** iUniverse offers distribution through the two largest distributors in the United States—Ingram, and Baker and Taylor—enabling readers to order and purchase your book from retailers around the world including Barnes & Noble and other booksellers. In addition, titles are available online through Barnes & Noble.com (www.bn.com), Amazon.com, BooksAMillion.com, and many other online sites. Authors who qualify for the iUniverse Publisher's Choice program may also be rewarded with the chance to see their books displayed in a local Barnes & Noble store.

- **Generous royalties.** iUniverse offers competitive royalty rates for all books sold through retail channels. In fact, our rates are higher than those offered by most traditional publishers.

- *Books in Print.* iUniverse titles are automatically listed in this important publishing resource used by booksellers, libraries, and researchers around the world.

- **Bookseller Discount Program.** As an option in the Premier and Premier Plus packages, authors can choose a 10 percent royalty in exchange for deeper discounts to retailers. Increasing the discount makes your book more attractive to booksellers and more rewarding for them to stock your book.

The Premier Plus Package

If you want your book to become a serious contender in today's competitive marketplace, and you're interested in publishing a book that meets the quality standards of major publishers and retailers, the Premier Plus package is the program you should consider.

Two exclusive features of this package are the Design Concept Evaluation—which provides you with the services of an experienced art director who ensures that your vision for your book translates clearly into precise instructions to the designer, is appropriate for the target audience, and meets book-industry standards—and the Cover Copy Polish, which ensures that the text on the front and back covers is appealing enough to motivate prospective readers to buy your book. Premier Plus also includes the all-important Editorial Evaluation—an expert third-party assessment of your manuscript designed to ensure that the quality of your work is consistent with your personal publishing goals.

Because Premier Plus is the only publishing package that includes evaluations of your book in three critical areas—editorial, design, and copywriting—it is the only package through which your book may become eligible for the iUniverse Publisher's Choice designation. Publisher's Choice enables your book to be displayed for eight weeks on the new paperback releases table in your local Barnes & Noble store.

Premier Plus Features

- Eligibility for Publisher's Choice
- Design Concept Evaluation
- Cover Copy Polish
- Editorial Evaluation with referral to Editorial Services
- Custom cover
- Inclusion in the iUniverse online bookstore
- Worldwide distribution through Ingram, and Baker and Taylor, and online booksellers such as Barnes & Noble.com (www.bn.com) and Amazon.com
- Marketing Success Workbook
- Marketing Toolkit
- Ten free paperback copies
- eBook formatting
- ISBN assignment
- One-on-one author support
- Nonexclusive contract

- Volume discounts for author book purchases
- Listing in *Books in Print*

The following options are available as add-ons to the Premier Plus package:

- Hardcover format
- Printed Bookselling Materials
- Press materials
- Kirkus Discoveries Book Review
- Co-op advertising opportunities
- Clipping service subscription
- Bookseller Discount Program
- Publicity Success Kit (for Editor's Choice titles only)
- Personal Publicist (for Editor's Choice titles only)

---

iUniverse was marvelous. I paid for the highest level of service plus the hardcover option. Once through the gate, I entered a wonderful and efficient organization. I was assigned a project manager who was as sweet and attentive as can be. They stuck to their demanding publishing schedule in an amazing way. The top-level package I paid for included a ten-page review, outstanding marketing support, and wonderful graphic arts support.

—Lt. Col. David Brown, USMC Ret.
  Author, *Battlelines*

The Premier Package

The Premier option combines our most popular publishing features into one affordable package. Along with the other important features offered as part of this package, you'll receive the Editorial Evaluation, which consists of valuable editorial advice from a seasoned expert, and the comprehensive iUniverse Marketing Success Workbook, which is chock-full of marketing and publicity tips.

If you are serious about your writing and are committed to making your book the best it can be, consider the Premier package.

Premier Features

- Editorial Evaluation with referral to Editorial Services
- Custom cover
- Inclusion in the iUniverse online bookstore
- Worldwide distribution through Ingram, and Baker and Taylor, and online booksellers such as Barnes & Noble.com (www.bn.com) and Amazon.com
- Marketing Success Workbook
- Marketing Toolkit
- Ten free paperback copies
- eBook formatting
- ISBN assignment
- One-on-one author support
- Nonexclusive contract
- Volume discounts for author book purchases
- Listing in *Books in Print*

The following options are available as add-ons to the Premier package:

- Cover Copy Polish
- Hardcover format
- Printed Bookselling Materials
- Press materials
- Kirkus Discoveries Book Review

- Co-op advertising opportunities
- Clipping service subscription
- Bookseller Discount Program
- Publicity Success Kit (for Editor's Choice titles only)
- Personal Publicist (for Editor's Choice titles only)

The Select Package

The Select publishing package is an economical choice for authors who need assistance with the basics of self-publishing. Books published under this package are available for purchase directly from iUniverse, either through our online bookstore or orders department, as well as through major online retailers including Barnes & Noble.com (www.bn.com) and Amazon.com. In addition, your book will be available for order through more than 25,000 bookstores worldwide.

Select Features

- Custom cover
- Inclusion in the iUniverse online bookstore
- Worldwide distribution through Ingram, and Baker and Taylor, and online booksellers such as Barnes & Noble.com (www.bn.com) and Amazon.com
- Marketing Toolkit
- Five free paperback copies
- eBook formatting
- One-on-one author support
- ISBN assignment
- Volume discounts for author book purchases
- Listing in *Books in Print*

The following options are available as add-ons to the Select package:

- Editorial Evaluation with referral to Editorial Services
- Cover Copy Polish
- Marketing Success Workbook
- Hardcover format
- Printed Bookselling Materials
- Press materials
- Kirkus Discoveries Book Review
- Co-op advertising opportunities
- Clipping service subscription
- Publicity Success Kit (for Editor's Choice titles only)
- Personal Publicist (for Editor's Choice titles only)

Coming off this season's NBC reality show *The Apprentice* with Donald Trump, I wanted to use the platform of publishing as a way to help others in their personal life and to support a charity that is near and dear to my heart—Autism Speaks. I chose the iUniverse Select package because it combined professional design, production, and distribution with lightning-fast speed to market. I was able to publish in time for the series finale. My iUniverse experience was second to none!

—Josh Shaw
   Author, *Who Invented Lemonade?*

The Fast Track Package

If economy and speed are important and full retail distribution is not a priority, the Fast Track publishing package may be your best option. Fast Track is especially suitable for authors who want to publish a book solely for their friends and family or who simply want the satisfaction of having a printed version of their work. As the most economical and streamlined self-publishing package available from iUniverse, Fast Track comes with the guarantee that your book will be ready for order in thirty days or less. For your book's cover, you'll get to choose from a variety of attractive templates. And, as with all iUniverse titles, your book will be offered for purchase on the iUniverse online bookstore. Available only for manuscripts submitted via the iUniverse Web site, Fast Track is a no-frills publishing package that gives you an attractive and professional-looking book within a matter of weeks.

Fast Track Features

- Inclusion in the iUniverse online bookstore
- Your choice of cover design from a number of professional templates
- One free paperback copy
- ISBN assignment
- One-on-one author support
- Nonexclusive contract
- Volume discounts for author purchases

Because my mom, Nancy Buck, was quite ill, we chose the Fast Track package to publish *The Poetry Corner,* her collection of poetry. The project took less than three weeks from start to finish (just thirteen business days), in large part because of the sensitivities of your employees and their abilities to work miracles. Of all the heartwarming memories I have of my late mother, seeing her reaction to having the book in her hand was the deepest of all.

—David Buck
   Documentary Filmmaker

The Back-in-Print Package

If you are a published author whose title is no longer available for readers to purchase, iUniverse can get—and keep—your book back in print.

iUniverse is the world's leading publisher of previously out-of-print titles. Through our Back-in-Print package, authors and agents of out-of-print titles can reconnect with readers quickly and economically. In as little as thirty days, your out-of-print book can be back on the market and earning you a 20 percent royalty on every sold copy.

iUniverse waives the publishing fee for members of the American Society of Journalists and Authors (ASJA), the Harlem Writers Guild, and the Authors Guild who publish through this program.

Back-in-Print Features

- Custom cover
- New ISBN assignment
- Inclusion in the iUniverse online bookstore
- Worldwide distribution through Ingram, and Baker and Taylor, and online booksellers such as Barnes & Noble.com (www.bn.com) and Amazon.com
- Marketing Toolkit
- Listing in *Books in Print*
- One-on-one author support
- Nonexclusive contract
- Volume discounts for author purchases

The following options are available as add-ons to the Back-in-Print package:

- Editorial Evaluation with referral to Editorial Services
- Cover Copy Polish
- Marketing Success Workbook

- Hardcover format
- Printed Bookselling Materials
- Press materials
- Kirkus Discoveries Book Review
- Co-op advertising opportunities
- Clipping service subscription
- Publicity Success Kit (for Editor's Choice titles only)
- Personal Publicist (for Editor's Choice titles only)

When my publisher, Knopf, decided to put *Bluegrass Conspiracy* out of print, I turned to iUniverse to take advantage of their Back-in-Print program. The iUniverse version has sold well over 10,000 copies and is still going—in fact, it's still one of my best-selling titles. iUniverse really has made the term *out of print* obsolete.

—Sally Denton
   Author, *The Bluegrass Conspiracy*

CHOOSING THE RIGHT PUBLISHING PACKAGE

If you're still unsure of which publishing package best fits your needs and goals, use the following table to compare the features and benefits of all the iUniverse publishing packages at a glance. Then determine whether the Premier Plus, Premier, Select, Fast Track, or Back-in-Print package is right for you. Once you do, continue to the next chapter, which will take you through each step of the iUniverse publishing process. Now—at last—you can get published!

PACKAGE FEATURES	Premier Plus $1099*	Premier $799*	Select $499*	Fast Track $299*	Back-In-Print
ISBN assignment	●	●	●	●	●
Worldwide distribution	●	●	●	◆	●
Publishers Choice eligibility	●	◆	◆	◆	◆
Editorial Evaluation with referral to Editorial Services	●	●	○	◆	○
Design Concept Evaluation	●	◆	◆	◆	◆
Bookseller Discount Program	●	●	◆	◆	◆
Volume discount for authors	●	●	●	●	●
Number of free paperback books	10	10	5	1	0
Nonexclusive contracts	●	●	●	●	●
Quick availability	●	●	●	●	●
Custom cover	●	●	●	◆	●
Template cover	◆	◆	◆	●	◆
One-on-one author support	●	●	●	●	●
iUniverse online bookstore inclusion	●	●	●	●	●
Listing in *Books in Print*	●	●	●	◆	●
eBook formatting	●	●	●	◆	◆
Hardcover format	○	○	○	◆	○
Marketing Toolkit	●	●	●	◆	●
Marketing Success Workbook	●	●	○	◆	○
Cover Copy Polish	●	○	○	◆	○
Printed Bookselling Materials	○	○	○	◆	○
Co-op Advertising Opportunities	○	○	○	◆	○
Kirkus Discoveries review	○	○	○	◆	○
Clipping Service subscription	○	○	○	◆	○
Press materials	○	○	○	◆	○
Publicity Success Kit (For Editor's Choice titles only)	○	○	○	◆	○
Personal Publicist (For Editor's Choice titles only)	○	○	○	◆	○

● Included in package price   ○ Optional service available for an additional fee   ◆ Not available with this package

*Please visit our Web site, **iUniverse.com**, or call **1-800-AUTHORS** for the most up-to-date information on pricing and eligibility.

Chapter 10

FROM MANUSCRIPT TO

PUBLISHED BOOK

iUniverse provides all the services you need to self-publish—book production, cover design, editorial services, publicity and marketing, and distribution—as well as the time-to-market benefits associated with print-on-demand technology.

This chapter lists the steps you'll need to take to make your dream of being published a reality.

STEP ONE: MAKE THE CALL

Whether you are several months from completing your manuscript or ready to publish right away, the first step to getting published is to visit the iUniverse Web site (iUniverse.com) or call us at 1-800-AUTHORS. Once you contact iUniverse, you'll be assigned a *publishing consultant*, who can answer your questions and guide you through preparing your manuscript for submission.

During your initial telephone conversation, your publishing consultant will review the features and benefits of each publishing package available through iUniverse as well as any additional services, programs, and promotions we offer. (See Chapters 7, 8, and 9 for more information.)

Be prepared to share your publishing goals—including your budget and desired timeline—so your consultant can help you determine the appropriate way to publish your book through iUniverse.

Beginning with this initial phone call, our contact-management system will be able to continually track the status of your account. In the unlikely instance that your personal consultant is unavailable to take one of your calls, any one of our highly qualified consultants can pull up the status of your account and assist you with whatever questions or immediate concerns you may have.

STEP TWO: SUBMIT YOUR MANUSCRIPT

iUniverse offers an online submission process, outlined in easy-to-follow steps. Or, if you prefer, you may take advantage of our submit-by-mail option. Guidelines for how to best prepare your manuscript, including an editorial style guide and a handy submissions checklist, are available online and in the appendix at the back of this book. By following these guidelines, you can help us publish your book as quickly and as professionally as possible. As you go through the submissions process, your consultant will be available to answer your questions about manuscript preparation or, if you're having problems with the online submission, refer you to one of our technical specialists.

When you submit your manuscript online, one of the first things you'll need to do is register for a myUniverse account, which provides you with a secure way to submit your manuscript and allows us to share important information and updates with you during and after publication. Once you've created your myUniverse account, you can begin the simple five-step submission process.

If you're unable to complete your submission in a single session, there's no pressure or need to rush. Just save your work on our secure servers and return to the next step at another time.

Making Your Path to Publication Smoother

We understand that you're probably eager to get your book into print. Since each book is unique and each author has different needs and goals, however, we cannot establish firm publication dates for authors up front; some projects simply take longer to complete than others. In addition, as with every other aspect of supported self-publishing through iUniverse, the author ultimately has the control, and because no two authors are alike in terms of personal schedules, marketing and editorial goals, and publishing needs, each timeline inevitably differs. For example, an author who is retired or whose sole career is in writing and publishing would probably be able to turn around author proofs more quickly than one who holds another full-time job and must work on a book during off-hours.

As a rule of thumb, however, think in terms of thirty-sixty-ninety: thirty days to produce a book via the Fast Track package, sixty days for a book via the Select package, and ninety days for a Premier or Premier Plus title. Editorial or design services may take additional time, but keep in mind that these are weeks well spent in creating a refined, professional book.

In short, while iUniverse is devoted to doing whatever we can to help you publish your book efficiently, much of the process also requires prompt action on the part of the author. If you do require a firm publication date, you can help expedite the process by paying close attention to our submissions guidelines, and doing your best to meet the dates we set for returning your proofs. Moreover, the better you've prepared your manuscript from the start, and the more you work with us to keep your schedule, the smoother your path to publication will be.

STEP THREE: GET PUBLISHED

As soon as we receive your manuscript, the publishing process kicks into high gear. First, we assign your manuscript a unique ISBN (International Standard Book Number) for each book format you want produced (for example, if you choose the hardcover option, that edition receives a separate ISBN).

Within a day or two of completing your submission, you'll receive an e-mail introducing you to your designated *publishing services associate*, which we refer to as a PSA. Your PSA is an expert in the publishing process at iUniverse who has the knowledge to efficiently guide you through every step of your book's production and publication. In other words, your PSA is your book's project manager.

Your assigned PSA will provide you with an overview of the production and publication processes and, from that point forward, will shepherd your manuscript through the following stages on its way to publication.

My publishing services associate truly went out of his way to help me in publishing two new novels with iUniverse. I was quite surprised at his willingness to walk the extra mile with me. This comes from a writer who has had eight books published by Doubleday and other top publishers. I just wasn't up to dealing with an agent and these traditional houses so I turned to iUniverse. Thank you!

—Jack Casserly
  Author, *Caesar's Coin*

Manuscript Qualification

Your PSA reviews your manuscript to ensure that it is correctly formatted and includes the necessary elements for your publishing package, such as graphics in the appropriate format and resolution, the author biography and photo, cover suggestions, and front and back cover copy.

After verifying that your manuscript submission contains all the necessary files, your PSA will send your book through the editorial and design stages applicable to your package.

Editorial Evaluation

If you opted for the Premier Plus or Premier publishing package, your PSA will send your manuscript for an Editorial Evaluation, in which a professional reviewer assesses your work to ensure that it has fulfilled the basic requirements of a published book. (This step is also offered as an option in the Select package.) Within a couple of weeks, you will receive your completed evaluation.

If the editorial evaluator provided an Editorial Rx Referral (which recommends a specific editorial service to enhance the quality of your manuscript), and you agree with the advice, you can choose to purchase editing through iUniverse, hire an outside editor, or do the work yourself.

If you choose to employ an editorial service provider from our established stable of professional industry editors, your PSA will advise you of your fee and send your manuscript to our editorial department. Once the editing is finished, you have the chance to review the changes made by the editor and to choose to follow or reject any editorial advice or recommendations given. Premier Plus authors have the added advantage of two important services—the Design Concept Evaluation and the Cover Copy Polish.

Cover Copy Polish

The text on the cover of your book—front and back—can make or break a prospective reader's buying decision. In addition, the keynote is a critical tool that helps in the development of a clear, concise sales and marketing handle and is used to pitch the work to booksellers, the media, and eventually directly to the consumer. If you select this option, a marketing professional will assess your title, subtitle, and any additional front cover copy, and will polish your back cover copy, author bio, keynote, and key search words.

Design Concept Evaluation

Although we provide a unique custom cover for all Select and Premier authors based on the art you provide or request, in the Design Concept

Evaluation—which occurs after your Editorial Evaluation and Cover Copy Polish are completed—an independent design evaluator who has extensive experience in traditional book publishing ensures that the ideas you have for your cover not only represent your vision but also meet retail bookselling standards. The design evaluator may recommend changes or improvements to your original cover concept, but we leave the final decision up to you.

Layout and Formatting

Once you provide us with a final version of your manuscript—which may include revisions you have made in response to the Editorial Evaluation and, if applicable, to one or more of the Editorial Services—your book moves into the production department, where the cover and the interior (called the *book block*) of your book are designed.

If you submitted via the Premier Plus package, you would have had the opportunity to participate in the design of your cover earlier in the process by reviewing recommendations from one of our professional design evaluators and providing feedback. As part of the Premier Plus, Premier, and Select publishing packages, a professional designer will create a custom front cover based on your ideas, incorporating any photographs or graphics you may have provided. If you opted for the Fast Track publishing package, you may choose a front cover design from our wide selection of attractive and eye-catching templates.

During the layout stage, while one designer creates your cover, another designer works on the interior of your book by formatting the page layout and by selecting an appropriate typeface for each of the textual elements such as the body text, headings, subheads, and chapter titles.

iUniverse is responsible for creating the interior and exterior design of your book, but you can help this stage of the process go more smoothly by following our submissions guidelines that govern graphic elements. Make sure that any photographs or illustrations you submit are the appropriate size, format, and resolution. As always, if you are uncertain about anything, ask your PSA for help.

The final interior and cover designs go to an iUniverse quality-control group, which ensures that the computerized files will be technically acceptable to the printer and that all of the mandatory book elements are included and complete. At this stage, iUniverse sets the retail price of your book based on the final page count.

Post-Production Revisions

Approximately two weeks after the production of your book begins, you will be able to view *proofs*—or electronic files of your formatted cover and book—and notify us of any final revisions you want made before your book is printed. Revisions at this stage may consist of minor editorial adjustments for such things as typos and small grammatical errors, and the addition of an index.

Proofreading

Reviewing your proofs will be your final chance to make sure that your book is error-free, so it's important that you take time to carefully review each page. If you choose to do the proofreading yourself, your PSA will provide proofing instructions along with an iUniverse proof form. Keep in mind, however, that it's difficult for authors to see typos and other errors in their own work, because they're simply too close to the content; that's why we offer and recommend professional proofreading services for authors who previously received the appropriate level of editing from iUniverse.

As a part of the proofing process, authors may make up to fifty minor corrections to their book cover, book block, or a combination of both—free of charge. Authors who wish to make more extensive corrections can do so for a nominal fee.

Once you or a professional proofreader have specified the necessary changes on the Electronic Proof Form, your PSA will send the form to our design team, who will implement the revisions. At that point, an iUniverse quality-control staff member will re-review your book. Then we'll let you see another proof so that you can be sure your corrections were made appropriately.

Index Preparation (for Qualified Nonfiction Books)

An index maximizes the usability of a nonfiction title but can be prepared only after the final proof corrections have been made to the formatted book, which gives the exact page numbers of the final book.

When you purchase our Indexing service, a professional indexer reviews your final page proofs to create a two-level index (containing main entries and subentries) tailored to your book's subject matter and potential audience. See Chapter 7 for more on the Indexing service.

Printing

After you approve your final proofs and, if applicable, send us your completed index, we'll send the appropriate files to the printer. Within weeks, you'll receive a shipment of author copies, and the electronic and print versions of your book will become available for direct purchase through iUniverse, selected retail outlets, and online booksellers, as determined by your publishing package.

Wow. Working with iUniverse has been a great experience. It's not often that online services deliver what they promise, but iUniverse has delivered beyond my expectations. For a first-time author, it has been not only an easy system but also a great educational tool. Your assisted support removes any concerns about the process.

—S. G. Bell
   Author, *The Magic Islands*

BEYOND PUBLISHING

Your book's publication doesn't mark the end of your journey. If your goal is to build a wide readership, you're just beginning another leg of the trip—marketing and publicity, which we'll cover in the next chapter.

However, even if your intended audience is limited to friends and family, you'll need to know the best ways to go about ordering your book.

Ordering

You may be tempted to order books as soon as you get your author copies in the mail, but you'd do well to wait until you've reviewed and approved these copies before ordering more. If you find anything you want to alter in your book at this point, you have to pay a minimal fee, but it is less embarrassing to catch and change serious errors now, rather than later—after you, your family members, your friends, your coworkers, and other readers order more copies.

One of the benefits of publishing through iUniverse is that there is no minimum-purchase requirement—if you're satisfied with the number of free copies that you receive with your publishing package, you'll never have to order another copy. If you choose to purchase additional copies, you can order them as you need—even one at a time. That's the advantage of print-on-demand.

Many iUniverse authors choose to order an initial quantity of their books to use for marketing and publicity purposes, to sell at author events, or to give as gifts. iUniverse offers significant quantity discounts to authors based on the number of copies of your book you purchase. (Find ordering information and our discount policies in Appendix C.)

Shopping and Ordering in Online Bookstores

All iUniverse titles are available for purchase from the iUniverse online bookstore. In addition, titles published through our Select, Premier, and Premier Plus packages may be purchased online at Barnes & Noble.com (www.bn.com), Amazon.com, and dozens of smaller online retailers.

Shopping for an iUniverse title online is no different from shopping for any other book on the Internet. Pull up the Web site of the book retailer (for example, Barnes & Noble at www.bn.com) and enter the title of your book, your name, or your book's ISBN. Within seconds, the cover of your book will appear on the screen along with the price and ordering information. The screen format is identical to those of other books for sale online from any other publisher—large or small—with nothing to indicate that your title is self-published or that it will be printed on demand. To order, just click "Add to Cart." Most iUniverse titles are printed and shipped within twenty-four hours of receipt of an order.

Special Ordering through Local Bookstores

If you have ever gone into a bookstore looking for a particular title that wasn't on the shelf, then you probably already know about special orders. You may have asked a staff person about the title, who told you that the book was not in stock but that it could be ordered for you. Because there are more books than there is retail shelf space to stock them, many books need to be special-ordered this way from the retailer.

If you published through any of our packages except Fast Track, your book will be available for special order through brick-and-mortar bookstores. Large bookstores such as Barnes & Noble have customer service desks where customers can place orders. In most cases, your book will be available for pickup within days.

It's easy for readers to order your book at Barnes & Noble. They simply go to the customer service counter and tell the clerk that they want to order a book that's not in stock. The clerk will look up your book in the Barnes & Noble title database and place the order. The customer will receive a call from Barnes & Noble when the book arrives, usually in about three to five days.

Using Ordering Options to Sell Your Book

In the next chapter, we'll show you how to take advantage of your ordering options, including author discounts, to help you generate interest for your book and earn more on every copy you sell. In addition, you will learn techniques for maximizing publicity for your book and creating a realistic, usable marketing plan that will further propel your book to success.

I chose to publish through iUniverse because I believed that no traditional publisher could get me to market faster with a high-quality product. I was not disappointed. My book was available around the world within three months of signing up for your program. I have friends in Japan and the UK that have been able to get my book though their foreign channels. Your distribution network is exceptional. I have nothing but praise for your process.

I believe that your company represents the future of publishing.

—Robert Tevis
  Author, *Keep Your Hands Out of My Pocket*

Part 5

GET NOTICED

Chapter 11

DEVELOPING AND IMPLEMENTING
A MARKETING PLAN

It took time, hard work, and money. Some days it seemed as though you'd never arrive. But, finally, you did—you made your dream of being a published author a reality. Now it's time to reach another dream—that of selling books. Before you can sell books, however, you need to market them.

To understand how marketing works, draw from your writing and publishing experience. Think about how far you've come since you had the initial idea to write your book. Most likely, your publishing success didn't happen overnight.

Similarly, marketing takes time. And as with any long journey, you should begin by planning and consulting a map. A marketing map can show you the most efficient route to your destination and point out the potential obstacles and detours along the way.

WHY DO YOU NEED A PLAN?

A marketing map serves several purposes.

- It is your road map to book-marketing success. It defines your destination, describes the people along the way who may buy your book, gives you direction on how to build that readership, and shows you how and where to go to reach each milestone.

- A marketing plan is a good scheduling and planning device that you can refer to daily to help you stay on your intended path, remain focused on important issues, and answer tough questions that you might otherwise avoid.

- A marketing plan also allows you to take an objective, critical look at your business, markets, and competition and to create methods to improve your sales.

- A well-drawn marketing plan can help convince a book buyer that you will drive customers into the store specifically to purchase your book.

iUniverse authors who achieve the Publisher's Choice designation, described in Chapter 8, need a marketing plan for another important reason: a Barnes & Noble buyer will closely review the plan when deciding where and when to stock a Publisher's Choice title. Although Publisher's Choice authors are guaranteed store placement in their local Barnes & Noble for eight weeks, a marketing plan that produces results can give authors exposure for an even longer period.

WHAT IS YOUR GOAL?

You can't create a map before knowing your destination. To gain at least a general notion of where you want to end up in your personal marketing journey, revisit the objectives you set during the writing process. The extent of those goals—however vague or specific you may have made them—will give you an idea how much work you will need to do and how much time and money you will need to expend in your marketing efforts.

For example, if your goal was to write a book for a limited audience of friends and family, you will be free to adopt modest efforts to get your book into your readers' hands. (If this is you, consider sifting out and practicing just a few of the most applicable steps from this chapter.)

If, on the other hand, you want to reach a large audience and achieve high sales, you must be willing to expend time, money, and effort in generous proportions.

Set Realistic Goals

Whatever your sales objective, the bottom line is this: set your goals within the realm of what is possible for you to accomplish. While you may yearn for a spot on the *New York Times* best-seller list or an appearance on *Oprah*, understand that those rewards are generally reserved for the authors of top-selling books put out by major publishers.

Once you have determined your goals, make them indelible by putting them in writing. Make them clear, so you do not later misinterpret their intent; specific, so you have no doubt about whether you achieved them; and attainable within a specified time, so you can measure them. Then arrange them from the most to the least important to ensure that you do the most important tasks first. Also, remember that while it's all right to dream big, if you set small, achievable goals, you'll be more motivated and able to reach them.

Finally, remember that establishing your sales and marketing goals is just the beginning—the foundation upon which your marketing action flourishes.

CREATING YOUR MARKETING PLAN

Once you've developed goals that are in sync with your ability to spend time and money on your marketing efforts, you're ready to start developing an actual marketing plan. Follow these three steps to creating a winning plan: position your book in the marketplace, know how to reach your target audience, and finally, assemble your marketing plan.

Step One: Position Your Book in the Marketplace

In Chapter 3, we encouraged you to visit your local bookstore to assess your competition and to help define your audience. If you followed our advice in that chapter, completing this first step will be easy. If you skipped over that part, you may want to revisit Chapter 3 and complete the necessary steps and checklists before moving forward.

Determine Your Target Audience

Before you can reach potential readers, you need to determine who they are. Many authors make the mistake of thinking that *everyone* is the audience for their books. Although that may be true in a sense for some books, trying to reach everyone is an insurmountable task. So start by identifying a core audience and build from there.

It helps if you can actually create a character in your mind that represents your ideal buyer. Use that image as your basis for developing a character or reader profile, then keep this profile in mind throughout your promotional campaign.

Next, answer these questions about the demographics of those you think will most likely buy your book:

- What is their age range?
- What is their gender?
- What is their income level?
- What is their education level?
- What leisure activities do they enjoy?
- What current events or issues are they discussing?
- What specific life events might they be facing (e.g., divorce, retirement, childbirth)?
- What magazines and newspapers do they read? What radio and television shows do they watch? What Web sites do they visit?
- What problems do they have?

- What joys do they experience?
- What organizations or associations do they join?
- What ethnic or religious group are they in?
- Where do they live?
- How can you reach them?

If you're unsure about the reader profile you've created, go back to the bookstore (preferably on a weekend, when bookstores have the most traffic) and watch the customers who browse in the section where your book would be shelved. Perhaps one of those customers perfectly resembles your reader prototype, or perhaps you'll find that you need to adjust the profile you created to better define your potential buyer. The more accurately you define your potential readers, the easier it will be to reach them.

Determine Your Geographic Focus

Geography plays an important role in consumer preferences. Some books are designed for urban audiences, while others appeal to rural dwellers. In fact, by analyzing the sales of competing books, retail bookstore buyers know exactly where a new book will most likely sell. Although you may not have access to sales data, you can project the areas that you think are most appropriate for your marketing efforts.

Position Yourself as an Authority

Once you have identified your audience and geographic focus, you need to position yourself to appeal to that particular audience. Develop a succinct author biography with no more than fifty words and make sure it contains these three key elements:

1. A few statements that communicate why you are qualified to write the book. Are you an expert in this field? What unique experience or insights do you have that give your book credibility? For example, "Jane Smith is the founder and president of *C-Cat*, the leading online magazine for ceramic cat collectors in the United States."

2. A statement that moves from your qualifications to something more personal. For example, "Her collection of ceramic cats now numbers more than 5,000." This personal information should relate to the book in some way.

3. Where you live and something about your personal life. You don't need to be specific; your listing can be as general as the state you live in, although including the city is also preferred (consumers often lean toward buying books by local authors). For example, "Smith lives with her husband, her three children, and her three real cats in Lincoln, Nebraska."

Remember, your aim is to convince potential readers that your book is worth reading; begin by convincing them that you are an author worth reading.

Assess Your Competition

Now that you've identified your target audience and where to find them, go to your local bookstore or search online to find books that compete with yours. To search online, pull up your favorite search engine and plug in key words that identify the subject of your book; these are the terms that potential readers will use to find your book. The titles that appear as the result of your search are most likely your book's competitors. But don't let your research stop there. Read and study the pieces to get to the heart of what makes these books competitive, then complete the following exercise.

Under the reader prototype you've developed, list three books that you think will compete most directly with yours. Then answer the following key questions:

- Why is your book different from the competition?
- Why is your book better than the competition?
- What do the other books have that yours does not?

Remember, the content of your book is not the only factor to consider when determining how your book is unique. Consider your credentials, as well. If you're a well-known expert in the subject matter of the book, for example, you will have an obvious advantage.

Identify Selling Points

Once you have some clear ideas of what makes your book outstanding, summarize these features into selling points. Selling points are brief, bulleted statements that summarize the features and benefits of your book. Aim to create about three to five selling points, but never more than ten. Your selling points should focus on what makes your book unique and what key factors make your book worth buying.

Remember that different aspects of your book may appeal to different audiences, so your selling points for one target audience might be different from your selling points for another.

Create a Hook

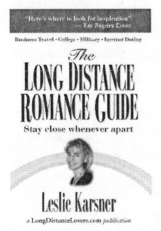

iUniverse author Leslie Karsner wrote *The Long Distance Romance Guide*. Her main hook: her book teaches couples unique ways to stay close when they are separated by geography. However, she also varies her hook depending on the type of potential reader to whom she's pitching. When talking to military personnel, for example, Karsner uses the angle that couples separated by tours of duty face stresses that go beyond simply being apart from each other; she then mentions that her book offers advice on handling such issues. When approaching college students, her hook is that young couples attending different schools have such a wide range of dating possibilities that they face a higher risk of infidelity—then she tells them they can learn preventive measures by reading her book.

Your selling points will be important components in the promotional materials you create, such as brochures, sell sheets, advertisements, and letters. To pitch your book to readers, however, you'll need something more concise and compelling—you'll need to summarize your selling points into a *hook*. A hook is a focused pitch that tells a particular person or group why they should take notice of your book. While a sales rep uses a hook to place a book with a retail buyer, and a publicist uses it to get media attention, you can use it to pique a potential reader's interest.

Before creating a hook, determine what your target readers are looking for. Then tailor your pitch accordingly, by tying your book into whatever your potential readers really care about. Here are some ideas:

- Use a local angle.
- Connect your book to a timely news story.
- Tie your book to a celebrity (but only if there's an actual tie-in).
- Use upcoming seasonal, charitable, or community events.
- Hit emotional hot buttons.
- Take a stand on a modern controversy or debate.
- Link your book to newsworthy anniversaries.
- Be generous—donate the profits to charity.

If you're having difficulty writing a hook, invite some creative friends over for a brainstorming session. There's no reason this should be a solitary task, and you might have more fun if you make it a group effort.

Once you've written your hook, the next step is to pare it down into a keynote.

Hone Your Keynote

Imagine you have only ten seconds to describe your book and convince someone to purchase it. The keynote, or "elevator pitch," which should consist of one or two sentences, succinctly tells readers what the book is about and why they should buy it.

When writing your keynote, be sure to avoid clichés or overused superlatives, such as, "This is the best book on..." or "This is the first and only book on..." You may compare your book to a well-known author, title, or film to give a reader a point of reference, but be realistic. Don't say, "This book is better than...[and name a mega-best seller]." Such comments usually amount to hype and will prompt most people to respond by rolling their eyes.

Here's an example of a well-presented keynote: "A veteran crime reporter delivers a gripping hardboiled whodunit with *Die Hard*-type action, set in modern Chicago. The emerging Russian Mafia and diabolical political overtones both figure into this edgy, thrilling plot."

Although many authors understandably find it difficult to condense a description of their book into one or two short statements, paring down your hook to a thirty-second keynote is essential to draw readers in. If asked to amplify, you can; but you'll lose your listener if you're not succinct at first.

Step Two: Know How to Reach Your Target Audience

Before you can pitch your book to prospective readers, you'll need to figure out how, when, and where to best reach them. Through the experiences and successes of the 18,000 authors we've helped to get published, iUniverse has learned the most effective ways to reach readers.

> Based on a wealth of author experience, iUniverse provides authors with a step-by-step approach for building an ever-widening reader base. When you follow the iUniverse marketing method, your success is not dependent on getting stocked in bookstores—you'll quickly learn easier and more effective ways to sell your book.

Although the following section includes ways to *implement* your marketing plan, wait until after you have *created* your plan before putting any of these steps into practice. For now, use these steps to become informed about the marketing processes that are available and to gather ideas about what methods might best help you achieve your goals.

Networking

Networking is interacting or engaging in informal communication with others for mutual assistance or support. Think about how this idea of mutual support applies to publishing: your book provides information or enjoyment to a reader, and in turn, you get satisfaction and earn royalties when the reader purchases your book. For an author, nothing is more important than or as potentially effective as the art of communicating with others to garner sales for a book.

Even authors with a small target audience need to network. Think of networking as a series of concentric circles, with each successive circle being larger than the one before it. When you let your family and friends know that your book has been published, you've formed the smallest networking circle. Professional acquaintances are an example of a group that could make up the next-larger circle. Members of your immediate community, such as those you communicate with through church, social, or sports organizations, can form a larger one still. Total strangers represent the widest circle, and the one that is the most difficult to reach. The more aggressive your marketing goals, the broader the networking circle you need to develop.

The good news is that not all networking has to be done by you. Once you get started by networking in smaller circles, your efforts can gain momentum and grow into larger circles without any additional effort on your part. In fact, best sellers are born this way—by word of mouth. According to Laurence Kirshbaum, chief executive of Time Warner's book group, "Word of mouth is still much more important than any kind of advertising."[1] Every time a reader enjoys your book and recommends it to a friend, that reader starts a network. It's the combination

---

1   *Wall Street Journal,* August 15, 2005.

of a multitude of recommendations—multiple networks—that drives a book to the best-seller list.

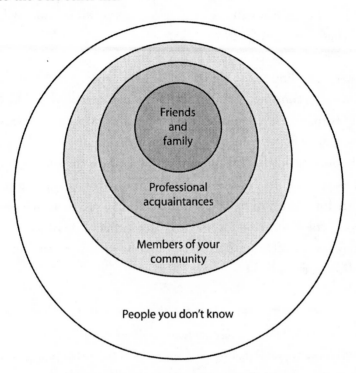

Friends
and
family

Professional
acquaintances

Members of your
community

People you don't know

**When networking, start with people you know and gradually
work outward to broaden your circle of influence.**

Garnering Endorsements

Although your primary goal for networking may be to sell books, successful authors also network to garner endorsements or testimonials. Having a reputable third party endorse you or your book can give you instant credibility—and thus marketability.

The key to landing valuable endorsements is to get quotes from recognized individuals or organizations, preferably those related to the subject of your book. If someone agrees to write an endorsement, you might offer to write a draft for his review and revision. You'd be surprised at how many people are happy to let you do the work for them. Drafting the endorsements yourself enables you to highlight different aspects of your book through different quotes. Be professional and avoid exaggeration in the quotes you write, and your endorsers will be more willing to accept what you've provided.

Once you've gathered multiple endorsements, keep an ongoing list and rank them according to the highest praise or the most well-known source, so that you can continually add or rearrange quotes as needed. The beauty of POD is that it allows authors the chance to update their books more easily and affordably to include additional or important endorsements. But, of course, your book isn't your only platform for sharing endorsements; endorsements also add credibility to media kits and printed sales pieces, so don't forget to update your marketing material as well.

Finally, enjoy your endorsements. Read them whenever you need encouragement—they are a great reminder of what you've accomplished by publishing a book.

Publishing with iUniverse has made my writing available literally around the world—from book signings and speeches in the US to publicity interviews in the UK, a lecture tour in Slovenia, and reader feedback from Qatar—and it's all happened in less than a year.

Doesn't get much better than that.

—David Henderson
  Author, *Making News*

Scheduling and Hosting Events

Most published authors will tell you that events represent a terrific and lucrative way to sell books. By scheduling or hosting an event, you're creating a reason for people to come together.

When most authors think of events, they think of book signings. You might expect that if you're in the bookstore with stacks of your book on display, strangers will be compelled to meet you and purchase an autographed book. In reality, there's too much competition in the bookstore, so you're better off scheduling an event in a location where you and your book can take center stage, and where you can make a compelling pitch to potential readers who are already inclined to be interested in your subject.

Here are three steps you can take to ensure that your events are successfully attended:

- Determine the places in which you're most likely to find your target audience. Clubs, reading groups, libraries, church meetings, schools, and coffee shops can provide ideal venues. Be sure that the location you chose is appropriate for your target audience.

- Plan a presentation, a reading, a seminar, or some other attention-grabbing activity to drive people to come and to make a purchase.

- Keep in mind that you need more than advertising to get people to attend your event—you need to be interesting, informative, or persuasive enough that people will fit you into their already busy schedules. This takes work, and there's no better way to do it than through aggressive networking.

Once you've learned how to bring people in, make your events as profitable as possible by considering the following:

- You're much more likely to sell books through direct interaction with readers than through indirect or impersonal methods. Even if the event is only loosely related to the topic of your book, people who enjoy your presentation might purchase your book so that they can "take you home." This is called *back-of-the-room* selling, which, if done consistently, can represent a significant income stream for many authors.

- iUniverse enables you to purchase your books at significant discounts; the more copies you purchase, the larger the discount you'll receive. If you hold an event outside of a bookstore—in a library or at a club, for example—buy your own books in bulk at a substantial discount, and then resell them at the cover price so you make a profit on every copy you sell. You can order copies online through a special iUniverse Web site that is available only to published authors, or you can always call your orders in to our toll-free number. More information is provided in the appendix at the back of this book.

If you're worried that you don't have the presence or the ability to do well at an event, remember, you don't have to be a professional speaker or a celebrity to be a good host. Just build events within the framework of your experience and personality. Start small and conduct events regularly—in no time, you'll build the confidence you need to drive the sales you desire.

In addition, although you certainly have the best chance of selling books when you are in direct contact with your readers, it might help you to know that events are no longer limited to physical, face-to-face interactions. The Internet has opened up a whole new world of opportunity for designing and hosting effective *virtual* book events—but we'll get into that in the next chapter.

Getting Media Publicity

Publicity is the most economical and effective way to reach the widest possible audience. Publicity involves contacting the media and convincing editors, reporters, producers, and talk-show hosts that featuring a story about your book will interest their audiences. Good publicity can spread a message quickly for a low cost, and selecting the right media can carry your message to a targeted audience.

Getting good publicity can be difficult, however. Media people are inundated with pitches from well-intentioned authors who hope to have their stories told. If you want to be taken more seriously, you'll need to create a professional media kit to present to media contacts. iUniverse authors whose books achieve Editor's Choice status can receive detailed instructions for preparing a media kit along with other valuable publicity tips, in our Publicity Success Kit. Editor's Choice authors can also hire, at an affordable rate, an iUniverse personal publicist to work for them. (These services are described in Chapter 7.)

Before you approach the media, you may need to tailor that hook and elevator pitch you developed earlier. Good or bad, most radio and TV coverage revolves around current issues, disasters, celebrities, sex, crime, violence, or heart-wrenching human-interest stories. So if you want to grab the attention of the media and their viewers, listeners, and readers, you'll need to give your hook a slant that ties it into current news.

Once you have a professional media kit and a prepared pitch, get in touch with media contacts through these three major publicity outlets:

1. *Print.* If you have a good story to tell, you can garner interest from newspapers and magazines. Getting a print article is much more effective than buying an advertisement in the same publication, because an article is an implied endorsement that adds credibility to your work.

   When most authors contact print media, they focus on getting book reviews. In reality, only a small percentage of traditionally published books gets reviewed—in fact, *Kirkus Reviews*, one of the review services most highly regarded by libraries, selects and reviews only 5,000 titles per year, or less than 3 percent of the nearly 200,000 titles published in 2004. For a self-published author, it is even more difficult to garner reviews, but it's certainly possible to get articles in the same newspapers or magazines that publish reviews. Likely sections to feature your book are those that cover the subject matter of your book, for example the science or education sections, or those that focus on local issues and people. This type of publicity, called *off-the-book-page* attention, is highly effective in reaching an interested readership.

2. *Radio.* Radio interviews may be easy to secure, because many stations are often hungry for content. With radio, practice makes perfect, so start with stations in your local area that have low bandwidth and a narrow reach. Make sure that you prepare a professional, compelling pitch, as well as a few key points that you want to get across—and don't let the interviewer take you off-course. iUniverse can help

qualified authors with interviews by offering media training and assistance in perfecting their hooks.

3. *Television.* Most authors dream about getting on a major talk show such as *Oprah.* In reality, national talk shows focus on celebrities and feature topics with wide appeal, and book publicists know it can take months—even years—to get an author on a show. Even if you are fortunate and patient enough to secure a television appearance, realize there's a big leap between making people aware of your book and persuading them to buy it. Conduct a simple experiment: for several days, watch for authors on national morning talk shows. How many are celebrities? How many of those books will you actually go out and purchase? Getting on a talk show may make you a celebrity of sorts, and it will definitely make people aware of you, but it won't necessarily help you sell books.

As with radio bookings, pursue television appearances by starting small. Local talk shows may be more willing than national or even regional programs to schedule you, and if they do, those appearances can help you become more comfortable in front of a camera—that way, if the opportunity arises, you'll be ready to move on to bigger programs. And as painful as it may be, record and watch tapes of your appearances so that you can fine-tune your approach for the next interview.

My iUniverse publicity campaign gave me the opportunity to speak on a variety of radio programs, which has improved my public speaking skills and my ability to think on my feet. As a result, when I am asked to speak (which is quite regularly), I feel equipped and knowledgeable enough to accept the challenge.

—Cathy Sultan
   Author, *Israeli and Palestinian Voices*

Advertising

Advertising can reach many consumers simultaneously and, depending on the circulation of the medium, can do so at a relatively low cost per exposure. It can increase awareness of your book and educate people about the benefits of buying it. However, advertising alone will not directly result in book sales. Think of your own experience: how many product advertisements do you see, hear, or read each day? And out of those ads that you're exposed to, how many of those products do you actually purchase? Because the return on advertising expenditure is not immediate, iUniverse recommends that you use advertising in conjunction with other, more direct ways to reach your readers.

On the other hand, you can get tremendous satisfaction from seeing your book on the printed page of a major publication—and further validation when one of your friends or colleagues notices the ad. If you choose to go this route, consider minimizing the cost of advertising in high-profile publications by taking advantage of the co-op programs available to iUniverse authors. Just be aware that because the benefits of advertising accrue over time, one co-op ad will generally not pay for itself.

Entering Contests

An award-winning book instantly receives a third-party stamp of approval that not even media attention can give, elevating it above the near 200,000 titles published every year. Potential book buyers, from salespeople to readers, prefer books that have been honored with a stamp of approval from a respected source. In addition, the organizations that hand out awards also promote their winning books by doing publicity for the winners and nominees. The iUniverse *Author Newsletter*, which is complimentary for all iUniverse authors, provides monthly information to help you enter as many contests and win as many awards as possible.

After failing to "crack the code" of commercial publishers, I decided to publish my religious nonfiction book with iUniverse. I am very glad that I did. I won a first place award in the 12th Annual *Writer's Digest* International Self-Published Book Awards and learned that making the effort is never really a waste of time. Hard as it may be to find markets for our ideas, it is not impossible.

—Art Lester
Author, *Seeing with Your Ears*

Attending Trade Shows and Book Festivals

A *trade show* is an event in which a group of specialized sellers display their products to a group of buyers. Attending book festivals and conferences is a great way to meet and network with other authors and, in some cases, sell books to the public. Hundreds, sometimes thousands, of industry people, including media people, potential customers, suppliers, and networking contacts, congregate at these expositions to look for new titles, information, contacts, and ideas.

A quick Internet search will yield a wealth of information on genre-specific or regional conferences that might be appropriate for you. If you find some you would like to attend, know that you do not have to exhibit at these shows to network with others; just attend them with your supply of business cards and copies of your book. Be careful not to be pushy, however. iUniverse is an exhibitor at many trade shows, and we know firsthand that an overly aggressive author can easily cross the line and become a nuisance. Be assertive yet considerate of people's time.

Step Three: Assemble Your Marketing Plan

Once you've carefully determined your marketing and sales goals, and have diligently reviewed the effective marketing strategies outlined in the previous section, you can move on to the third and final step: creating your marketing plan.

Combine the Elements and Find What Works

Apply what you've learned about the basic elements of author publicity and marketing to your goals to determine which methods will work best for you. Think about each method in more detail and jot down specific ideas or strategies for implementing some or all of these initiatives. Do research to find event venues, media vehicles, or conferences in which you're most likely to encounter your target readers.

The iUniverse Marketing Success Workbook, which is available to authors who publish through the Premier and Premier Plus publishing packages, provides tips and tools to help you to develop and refine your approach as you work to achieve your marketing goals.

Put Your Plan in Writing

You now have all the information you need to write a functional marketing plan. In its most basic form, your plan should provide summaries of your target audience, your competition, and your hook. It should also detail the specific marketing actions you intend to take as well as when and how you plan to take them.

If your goal is to sell only to your family and friends, your plan should be no more than a list of those people in your limited sphere of influence and a description of whether you will call, mail a postcard, or send an e-mail to each. If you seek broader and more potentially lucrative targets, your marketing plan should help you organize your time and your budget, and outline the specific steps you plan to take.

The iUniverse Marketing Success Workbook includes a useful marketing-plan template that shows you how to arrange elements in the proper chronological sequence and set a target date for accomplishing each item in your plan.

Time Your Publicity

In a well-coordinated marketing plan, timing is everything. Traditional publishers have that timing down to a science—newspaper articles, reviews, and commitments to television and radio shows are obtained months before a book is published, but they don't appear or air until after a book goes on the market. Everything is coordinated so that when the book goes public, readers are immediately able to purchase it.

Even if you go with iUniverse, which follows the demand-first model discussed in Chapter 6, timing is important, as you should be careful not to start marketing your book until it is fully available for order through online retailers and bookstores. iUniverse sends your book information and cover shot to retailers immediately upon publication, but because online retailers sometimes take several weeks to feed the information into their systems, it's best to wait at least three weeks after your book's publication before launching a marketing or publicity campaign.

iUniverse Publisher's Choice authors, in particular, need to time their marketing and publicity so that it occurs while their book is stocked in their local Barnes & Noble. Because this is so important, we offer Publisher's Choice authors special instruction and support in developing and timing their publicity efforts.

IMPLEMENTING YOUR PLAN: TAKING STEPS TOWARD SUCCESS

As you launch your marketing plan, remember that successful marketing is a marathon—not a sprint. If you try to accomplish too much, too soon, you'll burn out before you even get started. So take it slow and steady, and one step at a time.

As you begin to implement each step in your plan, remember to start small. The most successful marketing begins locally, expands regionally, and then grows nationally or even internationally, so always start by contacting people in your immediate geographic area. As you go, learn what works and what doesn't. Then, at each level, as you begin to experience success, let your campaign expand.

Chapter 12

MAXIMIZING SALES THROUGH
ONLINE MARKETING

If you are ready to grow your campaign to global proportions, or even if you're just getting started, one of the most effective marketing vehicles available is the World Wide Web. In fact, using the Internet is one of the promotional secrets of many successful iUniverse authors who, collectively, have sold more books than those at any other publishing services provider.

If you are not familiar with the Internet, the information in this chapter may initially seem a bit overwhelming. Our advice to you is this: become an Internet *user* before you become an Internet *marketer*. If you commit to spending one hour per day doing online research, browsing Web sites, and participating in online communities, you will quickly learn your way around the virtual community.

BENEFITS OF ONLINE MARKETING

The growth of the Internet has been a boon to authors and publishers, as it has presented new forums to find targeted groups of people, build awareness of books, and make purchasing fast and easy. Here are just some of the ways that online marketing can benefit authors:

1. **It eliminates geographical barriers.** On the Internet, like-minded people can find and communicate with one another in ways that they never have before. People with similar interests or tastes tend to join and participate in common online groups, which makes finding and reaching target audiences easier than ever.

2. **It is cost-effective.** The Internet is largely free, enabling you to reach large numbers of customers without spending time and money on traveling and advertising. For authors with ambitious goals and tight budgets, online marketing can help stretch dollars to achieve results.

3. **It is more convenient than other types of marketing.** Because very few book authors make enough money to support themselves solely through their writing, most have full-time careers and busy lives. On the Internet, you can market whenever you have a few minutes to spare, at any hour, and from the comfort of your home or office.

4. **It creates a lasting record of your successes.** The Internet is a giant content archive. Positive reviews, recommendations, and articles can last for years on the Web, which means people can continue to learn about your book well after you've finished your initial marketing push. And, if you're ever feeling a bit low, you can Google yourself to see a lasting record of your accomplishments.

5. **It is suited to less gregarious authors.** Many authors are uncomfortable with face-to-face selling. In fact, it's only natural that, as an author, you might prefer corresponding with people via e-mail and other written forms of communication. When you're online, you can reach out to strangers and develop relationships without the same fear of public speaking or direct interaction.

6. **It eliminates the necessity of bookstore stocking.** If bookstore stocking is so important, then why is Amazon.com the world's third largest book retailer?[4] The fact is that people are buying books online in increasing numbers and that every major brick-and-mortar retailer now has a significant online presence. By eliminating the need to physically stock books in order to sell them, the Internet has fueled the growth and acceptance of self-publishing.

Selling Books Online

Many publishing services providers charge extra or hidden fees to make your book available for sale to the public, but iUniverse automatically makes books available for sale through online bookstores at no additional cost to you. Plus, iUniverse offers an affiliate program that enables authors to earn an extra 10 percent on every book sold through the iUniverse online bookstore (more about that later).

The iUniverse Bookstore

The iUniverse Web site includes a virtual retail bookstore to make it easy for customers to purchase your book. Regardless of which publishing program you choose, your title will be available through the iUniverse bookstore for as long as you wish and at no extra charge. Our bookstore allows customers to find your book by title, author name, ISBN, key word, or subject. Best of all, your book will be featured on its own Web page, which displays the front cover, product details, marketing information, and links to your author bio and sample book pages.

---

4   In 2004, book sales of Barnes & Noble/B. Dalton totaled $4.45 billion; sales of Borders/ Waldenbooks totaled $3.37 billion; and sales of Amazon Media totaled $2.59 billion.

A page from the iUniverse online bookstore.

Other Online Bookstores

There's no greater thrill than holding your printed, published book in your hands, but seeing your book on an online bookstore such as Amazon.com or Barnes & Noble.com (www.bn.com) is the next best thing.[5] With all iUniverse publishing packages (excluding Fast Track), your book will be listed and available for purchase through online sites

---

5   Other examples include BooksAMillion.com, DealPilot.com, BookNook.com, and SmartBooks.com.

just a few weeks after you receive your author copies. iUniverse provides this service free of charge.

Your online book listing will look as professional as those of traditionally published books. Readers can post reviews online to further enhance your sales. In addition, iUniverse works closely with large retail partners to ensure twenty-four-hour shipment of your book—and we offer a 5 percent royalty bonus for every book purchased through the Barnes & Noble online bookstore.

The iUniverse Affiliate Marketing Program

To make online bookselling even more lucrative for authors, iUniverse offers the Affiliate Marketing Program. This program is offered through LinkShare, the largest affiliate-marketing network on the Internet. Authors who enroll in the program earn an additional 10 percent commission on iUniverse bookstore sales that result from online marketing. Therefore, if you plan to build a Web site or do online marketing, the iUniverse Affiliate Marketing Program provides a great way to help you recoup your publishing investment more quickly.

If you are familiar with HTML or are working with someone who is, becoming an iUniverse affiliate marketer is an easy, free, two-step process. Simply create a LinkShare merchant account. Once registered, you or your developer will gain access to iUniverse logos and banner ads, which you can add to Web sites or electronic mailings.

CREATING AN ONLINE PRESENCE

No matter how you publish, if you want to maximize book sales, creating a Web site—and then determining how to drive people to it—are essential steps. Your Web site doesn't have to be top-of-the-line, but it should contain content and features that will interest people in you and your book. Here are some tips for getting started.

Register a Domain Name

Your domain name is your site's address on the Web—the address that likely ends in *.com* or *.net*. It's inexpensive to register one or more domain names, so there's no need to wait until your book is published. Many Web services make it easy for you to get started, including Network Solutions and GoDaddy.com.[6] When you register your domain name, create a name that is easy to remember and that relates to your pen name or to the title of your book. Be careful that you don't get too complicated or too clever; a straightforward name is often best recognized and remembered by audiences.

Create Your Web Site

Once you have your Web address, the next step is to create your site. Unless you have lots of disposable cash, you don't need to invest in Flash or other programs to add fancy animation or sound features to your site. A simple Web site with solid content can serve your purpose. To get ideas for what to include in your site, browse the sites of best-selling authors, focusing on the content rather than the features.

There are many do-it-yourself kits for creating Web sites. In addition, many independent designers, as well as most of the domain registrars listed in the previous section, offer Web site–creation services. Many of these designers and companies will create multiple Web pages for less than $500. Sometimes large organizations offer special programs to their members with Web site templates for purchase.

Regardless of who creates your site, make sure the site is simple in appearance and easy to navigate. An image of your book's cover should be immediately visible, along with a brief summary and bullet points that list reasons readers should buy it. In addition, your author bio, reader testimonials, and endorsements should appear in plain sight and provide

---

6   Find a full listing of Web domain name-registration services at http://en.wikipedia.
    org/wiki/List_of_Domain_Registrars.

links to one or more online bookstores, to make it easy for customers to order your book.

Keep Your Web Site Current

One sure way to reduce your credibility as an author is to let the information on your site become outdated; most good Web developers give authors the tools they need to keep their Web site up to date. If your site lists your upcoming bookstore events, be sure to remove them once the dates have passed. Also, be sure to update your contact information and endorsements when necessary.

Generate Online Traffic

With millions of Web sites on the Internet, there's little chance that a reader will randomly stumble upon yours. You need to drive people to your site by referring to it in interviews, presentations, or mailings. Even better, give customers a reason to return after the first visit. Here are two popular Web features that authors use to keep their readers coming back:

1. **Podcasting.** Podcasting allows people to listen to, and sometimes view, whatever programs they want, whenever they want. In podcasting, producers record programs and make them available to anyone with a broadband Internet connection. Program listeners can then opt into free subscriptions by which they receive new audio or video files that are automatically delivered either to their computers, to their iPods, or to other portable audiovisual devices. Podcasting offers powerful opportunities for distributing information about your book because it harnesses the marketing power of the Internet but goes beyond Web pages and blogs, which are limited to text and images.

   In effect, podcasting allows you to become an independent producer of syndicated "shows" that promote your book. You can create one by recording interviews with readers over the telephone (with their permission) or by developing audio or video programs in which you are the only speaker. Your subscribers will have your show automatically delivered to their system and can listen to or watch it on their schedule. It's a combination of radio and TV—untethered from the clock and free of charge.

2. **Blogging.** A Web log, or *blog,* is an easily updatable Web site on which you can post information about yourself, your book, or other topics of general interest. A blog can substitute for a Web site or direct traffic to the primary Web site for your book. Web sites such as gather.com, blogger.com, typepad.com, and wordpress.com provide blogging tools that enable you to create a professional blog in little time. Once you've set up your blog, simply type in commentary, observations, insights, and other thoughts that relate to your book or its topic; visitors can read your material and add their own comments to your posting. Be sure to regularly update your blog with fresh, insightful commentary, relevant interviews, reviews, and links to other sites that relate to your book's topic and your audience's other possible interests.

HARNESSING THE POWER OF SEARCH ENGINES

Think about how frequently you use search engines like Google or Yahoo to quickly access information by typing in a key word. The listing of Web sites that appears as a result of your search does not turn up by accident; the companies or individuals who run those Web sites have most likely paid for a virtual connection to the key word you entered. If you have a Web site that features your book, you can take advantage of services that link Internet surfers to your title's Web site. Here's how a few of these services work.

Google Book Search

If you've been on the Internet much, you're probably familiar with the Google search engine, but you may not be aware of its Book Search program. iUniverse has partnered with Google to offer this program to interested authors. The program works like this: when readers search Google for a topic, title, or phrase, their search will bring up listings for all of the books that contain that search term in their titles or text. Each book listing, when clicked on, leads to a Web page that includes a synopsis of the book, any portion of text in which the search term appears, other selected pages from the book, and an option to immediately purchase the book from one of several online retailers. Because Google receives more than 200 million hits a day, Book Search provides a terrific way for authors to make their books visible to potential readers. Best of all, it's free. Learn more about Google Book Search at http://books.google.com/.

When you publish through iUniverse, you have the opportunity to opt into the Google Book Search program. Although iUniverse recommends participating, the decision is up to you.

Search-Engine Key Words

Pay-per-click (PPC) advertising is an effective, although potentially costly, way to find interested readers who use search engines. Services such as Google AdWords and Yahoo! Search Marketing enable you to bid on key words that relate to your book, which users may plug in when they do an Internet search.[7] When users enter the key words that you have purchased, their search results will include links to your Web site or to sites that sell your title.

Many iUniverse authors have purchased search-engine key words with great success. For example, Roger Chiocchi, author of the iUniverse Star title *Mean Spirits*, purchased the search term *ghost stories* the week

---

7   Learn more about these services at https://adwords.google.com and http://searchmarketing. yahoo.com.

before Halloween. Chiocchi watched his book reach number five on the Mystery and Thrillers Top Sellers list at Amazon.com.

Bidding on search terms can be expensive; if another entity wants those same key words to go to its site, the competitive bidding for the link can drive up the cost. Therefore, reserve your bidding for specific key words that have the potential to draw the most interested users to your site. Also, initially limit your purchases to one or two terms, until you determine whether such key-word targeting is effective enough for you to warrant the expense.

REVISITING THE ELEMENTS OF MARKETING

In Chapter 11, we discussed some of the methods that authors can use to generate sales: networking, landing endorsements, hosting events, getting media publicity, advertising, entering contests, and attending trade shows. Some of these methods can be easily adapted to online marketing.

Networking

As a giant network, the Internet provides the perfect vehicle for authors to announce a book's publication to people they know and to develop relationships with people they don't know. Both of these opportunities are important for successful book marketing.

Networking with People You Know

The simplest way to begin marketing your book online is to send an e-mail announcement to everyone you know and have known. Start by creating a mailing list. You may be surprised at how many people you can reach if you include friends, family members, neighbors, coworkers, industry colleagues, schoolmates, alumni, and church members, as well as acquaintances from business associations, clubs, and groups to which you belong.

When you compose your announcement, be careful to avoid using provocative or exclamatory words in your subject line, which may result in your e-mail getting deleted by the recipients or even automatically blocked by their servers. The content of your e-mail should be enticing but not too sentimental or shocking—don't create chain letters that threaten financial loss or ill health if the recipient doesn't forward it. If you've written an interesting e-mail, friends and colleagues will automatically share it with others and won't need to be forced. Most of all, keep it *short.*

Also consider including an invitation to a virtual book-purchasing event in your announcement: ask everyone you know to purchase your book within a specified time window on the same date and include a link to the online bookstore that you'd like everyone to use. During the event, log on to your specified bookstore and have fun watching your sales rank climb. If you pick the right time, your book's sales rank might even climb to the top.

Networking with People You Don't Know

If you have broad goals for your book's success, you'll have to reach out to people beyond your close circle of friends and family to those who represent your broader target audience. By forming relationships with new people, you can begin to build word of mouth and sell books without ever needing to see them on a bookstore shelf. Here are some places to find your target readers on the Internet:

1. **Special-interest forums** are ideal for networking because they consist of people who share information on areas of mutual interest. These groups can help you expand your existing network and link you to like-minded people throughout the world. Special interest groups include discussion groups, newsgroups, bulletin boards, message boards, and chat rooms.[8]

---

8   Find a wide range of discussion groups at http://groups.yahoo.com/ and http://groups.google.com.

2. **Web sites related to your topic.** Search for Web sites with content that relates to your book by entering key words into several search engines. By spending time on those sites, you may find people who are interested in reading your book or can provide a positive review or recommendation. It will take patience and careful follow-up, but over time, you can develop a whole network of readers through Web site research.

3. **Webrings.**[9] A Webring is a community of Web sites united by a common interest and organized into a *ring* of mutual links. Webring users can easily surf from site to related site, visiting each one in the community. Webring links give you access to the list of member sites and allow you to add your Web site to the ring. This type of promotional activity is *targeted marketing* because you introduce yourself to people who are already focused on and interested in the subject matter of your book. Webrings can bring traffic to your site in two ways: from your site's listing on the hub page (the ring's homepage, accessible to general users) and from the *ring flow* (Internet traffic generated by the community).

4. **Electronic mailing lists** are interactive discussion groups in which registered members post e-mails on subjects of mutual interest. Some lists have moderators who screen the e-mails before posting them to the group. Before you attempt to market on an electronic mailing list, join one and become an active participant. Doing so will help you build a network of like-minded people.[10]

Scheduling and Hosting Events

As you expand your network, you might consider hosting or participating in online events. We already mentioned how an online book-purchasing

---

9   Go to http://dir.webring.com/rw for a directory of Webrings.

10   For example, PUBLISH-L (http://www.publish-l.com/) is an e-mail discussion list for issues related to publishing.

event for family and colleagues might prove beneficial, but there are many opportunities to make or create online appearances that will help you increase awareness of your book. Here are just a few.

Internet Radio Shows

As you become familiar with podcasting, you may happen upon Internet radio shows for authors. These shows are a collection of podcasts organized around a single theme. If you are ambitious enough, you might consider hosting your own show; alternatively, you could find Internet radio shows on which you could appear as a guest author.

Webinars and Webcasts

A Webinar is an interactive seminar or meeting conducted over the Internet. Just as many businesses use online meeting software to connect and communicate with customers, you can purchase easy-to-use software packages to create and host your own interactive seminars for targeted audiences. In contrast to the interactive nature of a Webinar, a Webcast is a one-way transmission of content. Many authors create and record online seminars, which they use to create ongoing Webcasts. As you gain popularity or credibility through public exposure on Webcasts, you may be invited to participate in other online chat sessions or Webinars.

Virtual Book Tours

Virtual book tours (VBTs) have recently become popular because they allow authors to connect their books with interested readers through blogs and other Web sites. On a VBT, you "stop" at any number of related Web sites within a given period. At these stops, you may be interviewed, take over a site blog for a day, or answer questions from readers. The key reason for the success of VBTs is that you can reach your audience through various channels in a condensed period to build awareness of your book.

Publicity

Although Web sites and online events can help generate media publicity, conversely, the most successful authors use traditional publicity to drive people online. As you give interviews and presentations, repeat your Web address several times and ask people to visit. Even better, give people a reason to visit: tell them about the free item you're offering or the contest you're holding for people who visit or register on your site.

As you become involved in media publicity, continually update your Web site by adding the most recent media clippings, interviews, and links to any publications, reviews, or general Web sites that mention your book. In time, you'll build a publicity archive that can help you establish credibility with new visitors—and provide you with a wonderful way to review and celebrate your success.

Putting It All Together

Remember, marketing, like publishing, is a journey—the more avenues you explore, the more likely you are to find the strategies that work best for you and drive your book to success. So don't limit yourself to either traditional or online techniques—the best marketing efforts combine both.

Chapter 13

DEFINING AND
CELEBRATING SUCCESS

Success is not the key to happiness. Happiness is the key to success. If you love what you are doing, you will be successful.

—Albert Schweitzer

It requires drive and perseverance to complete a manuscript, and it requires a sense of initiative to take control of the publishing process by doing it yourself. If you've gotten this far, all that's left now is to implement your marketing plan. With hard work and a little luck, you may make it to the top.

Realize, however, that while there's nothing wrong with dreaming big—most successful authors do—successful authors also match their hope and enthusiasm with two guiding principles: first, a commitment to work hard, and second, a willingness to accept and push through any disappointment that may occur along the way.

Although no one can predict what lies ahead for you, our extensive experience with self-published authors has given us invaluable insight on defining and celebrating success.

PLAN FOR SUCCESS

Before you can achieve success in any endeavor, you must define it in terms of your undertaking. The best way to do that is to focus on your goals.

In the beginning, as you embarked on writing your book, we emphasized the importance of setting goals that are SMART: Specific, Manageable, Attainable, Realistic, and Tied to time. As you move forward to implement your marketing plan, continue to set goals that are SMART. Only this time, instead of setting goals that revolve around how many hours you want to write per week or how many pages you want to produce in a day, relate your goals to how many sales you want to garner. Here are some SMART ways to set and meet your sales goals:

- **Be realistic, especially with regard to time and money.** You may aspire to be the next John Grisham, but is that possible for you? Tales of Grisham's tenacity and focus are legendary in writing circles. His first book, *A Time to Kill,* was handwritten on legal pads over a three-year period, during which time he also practiced full-time as an attorney and part-time as a Mississippi state legislator. Grisham wrote every day, getting up at 5:00 AM to scribble a few pages before going to work, and sometimes grabbing as few as thirty minutes between appointments or during downtime in the legislature to write a few more. Once completed, his manuscript made the rounds of sixteen agents before one would take him. It took another full year and more than two dozen submissions to sell the book, and even then, with an initial press run of 5,000 books, most of which Grisham marketed himself, *A Time to Kill* was no runaway best seller. It took his second and third books, *The Firm* and *The Pelican Brief,* to make John Grisham a household name. If you are willing and able to commit that kind of time and energy, you may have a realistic goal.

  Also, you must be able to put your ego on the shelf and ask yourself—and others—whether your book has the kind of quality readers are looking for. If you cannot honestly tell yourself that you are willing and able to both commit relentless time and energy, and swallow any pride of authorship, you may need to rethink your aspirations and, if necessary, scale back.

We've said this before, but it deserves repeating: marketing is not a sprint but a marathon. You might not win the race the first time out, but be patient and set realistic goals—eventually you'll get to where you want to be.

- **Identify incremental steps to achieve each goal.** A goal is the end result, the big picture. Keep your eyes on the goal, but not at the exclusion of seeing the road and the vehicle that can get you there.

  Break down your goal into segments that are within your control. Then divide each of those segments into incremental steps. Remember to make each step as specific as possible and to set deadlines for achieving each one. Little by little, you'll reach your destination. The goal-setting worksheet in Chapter 1 illustrates this concept.

- **Establish realistic benchmarks.** Although it's perfectly natural to want to reach for the stars, be careful not to aim so high that you set yourself up for failure. You'll experience more satisfaction and a greater feeling of accomplishment by setting smaller, more readily achievable goals. For example, instead of setting your sales goal in the thousands of copies, scale it back to hundreds. You may still sell in the thousands, but imagine how successful you'd feel if you exceeded your goal and broke the four-figure mark.

- **Understand the relationship between expectation and investment.** The more ambitious your expectations, the more money and time you must be prepared to invest in editorial excellence and marketing. Good books don't sell themselves; bad books don't sell at all. If you strive for sales numbers of four figures or more, your book must, first, be the best it can be editorially. Even then, it won't break any sales records unless you spend time and money to heavily promote it.

- **Commit to your plan.** Your vision of success is yours. You define success for yourself and determine how to achieve it. If you cannot fully commit to your plan, you cannot fully expect to succeed.

SMART
Goal Worksheet
Create a separate worksheet for each goal

Make every goal **SMART**:
S – Specific
M – Manageable
A – Attainable
R – Realistic
T – Tied to time

Goal:

Sell 250 copies of my book and qualify for Reader's Choice by December 31

Action steps:	Due date:
1. Do Google research to find four Web sites relevant to my target audience.	April 1
a. Contact two people who influence the content of each Web site and ask them to read the book and post a recommendation.	April 5
b. Identify three sites to which I can submit an article.	April 10
c. Find and join a special interest group related to my audience.	April 15
2. Develop a mailing list of high school, college, and former work contacts to inform them of book.	May 1
3. Hold launch party to sell forty copies.	July 10
a. Set date, venue, and theme.	May 15
b. Create invitations.	May 20
c. Address and mail invitations.	June 1
d. Finalize food, drink, party favors.	June 15
e. Write speech.	July 5
4. Prepare a media kit to be sent four weeks before event.	August 1
a. Write a media/press release.	July 10
b. Prepare a list of five to ten interview questions.	July 15
c. Create a list of fun facts or statistics related to book to pique interest.	July 15
d. Create a sell sheet to summarize book and author features.	July 15
5. Send a copy of the book and media kit to an alumni magazine.	August 1
6. Research potential event venues in local area and identify three possible locations.	August 15

- **Be patient—very patient.** Achieving your goals may take several years. Many authors market aggressively for six to eight weeks and then become discouraged when the sales don't roll in. Don't follow their lead. Although it makes sense to begin your marketing campaign strong to build early awareness, continuing your marketing efforts is equally important, even if you only commit to doing one or two things per week after the initial launch. A steady, persistent approach yields winning results.

LEARN FROM YOUR EXPERIENCE

Preparation and persistence can take you far. But if you're not careful to learn from your mistakes, you may find yourself going too far in the wrong direction. As you take steps to reach out to readers, market your book, and ultimately reach your sales goals, you'll have vast opportunities to learn—not only about publishing, but also about yourself. To stay on the right track, learn from your failures and celebrate even your smallest successes.

First, learn how to stay positive in the face of rejection and disappointment. When it comes to marketing, you can only make the public aware of your book; you cannot make them purchase it. Therefore, measure your success only in terms of things you can control—such as your own marketing actions and personal accomplishments—rather than in terms of sales. As you market, expect to get ten nos for every yes, but try to see each no as bringing you one step closer to the next yes. In addition, if you find your book isn't selling even after you've successfully generated reviews and publicity, know that you are in good company: sometimes even award-winning books from the most prestigious organizations end up with low sales.

Second, learn to be honest with yourself and to accept constructive comments from others. As painful as that may be in the beginning, you will end up a better author for it. Open your mind to learn from those you contact as you actively market your book. Don't merely push the book on them; ask for honest feedback. If you learn that your marketing techniques need revision, rethink your plan. If people tell you that there's a reason they're not buying the book, don't give up—think about making that revision or applying what you've learned to your next book. If you've done it once, you can do it even better the next time around.

Finally, learn to have fun. Publishing and marketing your book—although challenging at times—should, overall, be an enjoyable experience. If it ceases to be, it may be time to reassess your goals. Remember the epigraph of this chapter: if you love what you do, you will be successful at it.

If you stick with it and stay positive, you'll be able to look back on your experience one year from now and be amazed at how much you grew and learned from your personal publishing journey.

Throw a Party

Many authors refer to their manuscripts as their babies and liken the publishing process to giving birth. You've surely attended or hosted birthday parties before—most authors celebrate the publication of their books in a similar fashion, by hosting a party that launches the publication of their book.

Here are some tips for hosting a publication party that people will remember:

- Invite everyone who cares about you. They'll be delighted to celebrate your success with you, and may even ask to purchase an autographed copy.

- Incorporate a theme that relates to your book. Ask people to dress in costume or decorate around a theme that relates to the period or location in which your story is set.

- Instead of hosting a somber signing event, think of ways to make it fun. Hold a contest or game that relates to your book, for example, or invent a trivia game that requires people to answer questions about your book or to read excerpts aloud—then award the winner with a free copy.

- Select a fabulous location for the event. Public buildings such as museums, libraries, governmental offices, and structures in outdoor parks and recreation areas are quite impressive—and appropriate events are sometimes allowed in these venues for little to no cost. Alternatively, local suppliers might furnish food or beverages at reasonable cost, and sometimes even for free, if they think it will be well attended enough to possibly receive press attention. A local microbrewery or winery, for example, might be willing to host a party with tours of the premises; you'd get a wonderful location, and they'd get attention and, possibly, new customers.

- Use your iUniverse author discount to buy several copies of your title in advance, then offer to autograph books purchased during the party. Be sure to ask or hire someone to collect money and make change so that you can focus on signing books. If you sell each copy at list price, you might even make enough to pay for the party.

- Create a book-purchasing event before your party, in which you ask people to make online purchases. Then ask them to bring their copies to the launch for autographing. Remember to designate a single online bookstore, and ask them to buy the book on a specified date during the same one- or two-hour period. Then as you watch your sales rank climb, use your computer to make a "screen capture" every time the rank improves. (Ask a computer-savvy friend for help if you need to.) Put printed screen shots in an album or take them to your local printer to be blown up into posters, which you can display at the party. Or, if you did well enough, make your top rank the theme of your celebration. Who knows—you might be able to honestly claim best-seller status.

- Give a short speech at the party. Thank everyone for coming and for supporting you before, during, and after publication. Send people off by asking them to read the book and recommend it to their friends, or even to write a positive review on the Web site of their favorite online bookstores.

- Send your guests home with a token party favor. Such a gift can be as simple as candy wrapped with paper that has the cover of your book on it. Many local specialty advertising firms offer bulk deals on promotional items that you can use as giveaways.

- Ask a local organization, club, or church group that you're a member of to host the party. Organizations, even national ones, often are delighted to show appreciation to an active member or volunteer by bringing associates together to congratulate the author. This not only gives the organization a chance to recognize the author but also enables the group to attract positive attention from the community—and sometimes even from the press.

- After the party, create a publishing scrapbook made up of pictures you took at the celebration. Include congratulatory notes and e-mails, as well as news clippings or reviews that you gather as you market your book, to create a memorandum of your success and accomplishments.

Regardless of how ambitious your goals are or where your publishing journey takes you, treat yourself to a launch party to celebrate your new status as a published author.

I am so happy that, after being a professional writer all my life with almost every word I've written either printed or filmed, I finally had something that I wrote for myself—something intimately personal—become the first book I can actually hold in my hand. And, while it probably won't bring riches, I will have the joy of knowing that, with the help of iUniverse, it is being read by others.

—Chuck Maisel
    Author, *Majorca, Paradise Not Lost*

Enjoy Yourself

No matter how you define success, you will soon learn that achieving it, while challenging, is worth the effort. If you are willing to commit to a plan, focus on the goal, and learn along the way, the payoff can be huge.

So take pleasure in your journey toward the ultimate reward. This is your book, your success. Enjoy it.

Appendix A

GENERAL INFORMATION

If you don't find answers to your questions in the book or in these appendices, please contact one of our publishing consultants by calling 1-800-AUTHORS x504 or sending an e-mail to submission.inquiries@iuniverse.com. Our associates are available from 8:30 AM to 5:30 PM Central Time, Monday through Friday. Up-to-date fees for iUniverse services and publishing packages are available on our Web site: iUniverse.com.

PRE-SUBMISSION INFORMATION

Setting Up Your myUniverse Account

Before submitting your manuscript to be published, our online system will prompt you to enter your e-mail address and a password of your choice in order to become a registered user. Once your account has been established, you'll be able to submit your manuscript online. Your private myUniverse account enables you to track the sales of your book, purchase additional iUniverse products and services, and access the iUniverse Author Event Calendar. Be sure to make note of your password so that you can easily access your account as often as you wish. It is very important that you **create and maintain only one myUniverse account;** please do not set up a second account if you forget your password. If you should happen to forget your password, we will be happy to provide it to you upon request.

Forms of Payment

We accept Visa, MasterCard, Discover, and American Express charge cards, as well as money orders and electronic checks.

Submitting by Mail

While online submissions are preferred for all iUniverse publishing packages, iUniverse will also accept, for an additional fee, manuscripts sent by mail, when you publish via the Select, Premier, or Premier Plus publishing packages.

OCR Service

If you have a typewritten manuscript or a previously published book that you would like to convert to a word-processed document, our Text Scanning and Conversion service is available for a reasonable fee per page. We use optical character recognition (OCR) software to scan printed text and convert it into a digital file. You'll receive your manuscript on disk, in your choice of Microsoft Word, Corel WordPerfect, or Rich Text format.

iUNIVERSE POLICIES

iUniverse Content Guidelines

1. *Copyrighted and Other Protected Material*—iUniverse will not publish plagiarized material or books that violate or infringe upon any personal or proprietary rights, including copyrights, trademark rights, trade secret rights, contract rights, privacy rights, or publicity rights of any other persons; excerpted material longer than allowed by traditional fair-use practices or used without proper permission within the text or on a permissions/acknowledgments page; and song lyrics without proper authorization. Authors do not, however, have to credit or acknowledge sources for generic information that is known to the general public.

2. *Injurious Material*—Books cannot, in any other way, be illegal or include any recipes, formulae, instructions, or recommendations that may be injurious to any reader, user, or third person.

3. *Pornographic or Hate-Related Materials*—iUniverse will not publish works that are defamatory or prejudicial; or that are pornographic or obscene to a degree that they would not be carried by a traditional trade bookstore.

4. *Public Domain*—iUniverse will not publish works that are in the public domain.

Software Policy

To ensure the quickest and most accurate production of your book, please submit your manuscript as a single document in one of the following word-processing programs:

Windows: Microsoft Word 95/6.0 and above or WordPerfect 6.0

Macintosh: Microsoft Word 98 and above or WordPerfect 5.0 and above

Linux: Star Office/Open Office

Note: Presently, we do not accept Quark, InDesign, or PageMaker files.

Refund Policy

You may receive a refund of any submission fees before a submission enters the production phase. Once a submission enters the production phase, submission fees are non-refundable. For editorial, design, or cover copy services, no refunds will be given once the service has been initiated. You can check the status of your submission in your myUniverse account on the iUniverse Web site simply by clicking on *Submission History.*

FORMAT, PRINTING, AND PRICING

Length of Your Book

iUniverse can publish books that range from 48 to 740 pages. Fiction and nonfiction manuscripts should be between 10,000 to 244,000 words. The pricing model for print-on-demand is best suited for books under 500 pages, but extremely large books may be published in two volumes.

Trade Paperback

iUniverse books are printed in a perfect bound (also referred to as a trade paperback) format. The majority of our books are published in a 6" × 9" format. Other size options include 5.5" × 8.5", 7.5" × 9.25", 8.25" × 11", and 8.5" × 11".

Hardcover

In addition to including the standard trade paperback format in our publishing packages, iUniverse can produce your book in a 6" × 9" hardcover format, for an additional fee. The hardcover format features a durable cloth binding, an embossed spine, and a full-color dust jacket.

Other Bindings

iUniverse does not publish wire-o, plasticomb, three-ring, or spiral bound books.

Book Sizes and Paper Types

To ensure consistent print quality even as books are printed one at a time, iUniverse standardizes the paper used during printing. Below are the paper types used for the various book sizes we offer:

Binding Size and Format	Paper Weight	Paper Color	Extras
5" × 8" (interior)	55 lb.	Colonial White (Crème)	Acid-free, lignin-free
5.5" × 8.5" (interior)	55 lb.	Colonial White (Crème)	Acid-free, lignin-free
6" × 9" (interior)	55 lb.	Colonial White (Crème)	Acid-free, lignin-free
7.5" × 9.25" (interior)	50 lb.	White	Acid-free, lignin-free
8.25" × 11" (interior)	50 lb.	White	Acid-free, lignin-free
Paperback Cover	80 lb. cover	White Enamel	Full color, acid-free
Hardcover Jacket	100 lb. text	White Matte	Full color, acid-free

Book Pricing

Your book's price, which is based on the number of pages in your book, is determined once the manuscript has completed the production process. The following table provides you with an estimate of the cover price of your book. This table does not guarantee that your book will fall within this range; the final price is determined only once your manuscript has been submitted and gone through the production process.

Manuscript Word Count	Page Count*	Book Price Range*
20,000 (or fewer)	75 (or fewer)	$8.95 – $10.95
40,000	120	$10.95 – $13.95
60,000	180	$13.95 – $16.95
80,000	240	$15.95 – $19.95
100,000	300	$17.95 – $21.95
120,000	360	$20.95 – $23.95
140,000	420	$22.95 – $26.95
160,000	480	$25.95 – $29.95
180,000	540	$27.95 – $31.95
200,000+	600+	$29.95+

* Estimated page count and book price. Nonfiction books average $1–$2 more than fiction books with a comparable word count.

Appendix B

WHAT TO EXPECT—GUIDELINES FOR YOUR ONLINE SUBMISSION

Following is a preview of what we ask you to provide during the iUniverse online submission process and some tips to guide you through. Go to iUniverse.com for more information.

STEP 1: CUSTOMER PROFILE
Customer Profile

Contact information such as address, phone number, and e-mail address that will be used to correspond with you throughout the publication process.

Please provide all of the phone numbers where we can reach you—both during the day and in the evening. If your employer allows personal calls during business hours, please provide your work or cell phone number, so that we may reach you during the day.

Authors and Other Royalty Participants

The **name** of each individual or entity that will receive a portion of the royalties generated from the sale of your published book.

Sometimes, various people and organizations divide the royalties. For example, several co-authors may arrange to share royalties equally, or if one author contributes more to the project than the others, that writer may receive a larger share. Some authors choose to donate a portion of the royalties to a favorite charitable organization, while others have arrangements with literary agents who receive a percentage. This is a financial decision that only you can make.

The **type of royalty participant**, such as author, co-author, agent, corporation, or organization.

The **primary contact** that will be used for all publishing correspondence.

STEP 2: AUTHOR PROFILE
Author Biography (no more than fifty words)

The author biography should consist of three key elements:

- **A few statements that communicate why you are qualified to write the book.** Are you an expert in this field? What unique insights or experience do you have that give your book credibility? For example, "Jane Smith is the founder and president of *C-Cat*, the leading online magazine for ceramic-cat collectors in the United States."

- **A statement that moves from the qualifications above to something more personal.** For example, "Her collection of ceramic cats now numbers more than 5,000." This personal information should relate to the book in some way.

- **Where you live and something about your personal life.** You don't need to be specific; your listing can be as general as the state you live in, although including the city is also preferred (consumers often lean toward buying books by local authors). For example, "Smith lives with her husband, her three children, and her three real cats in Lincoln, Nebraska."

STEP 3: BOOK INFORMATION
Information about Your Book

Title
Select your title carefully so that it either relates clearly to the content of your book or has a clever connection. Often the title and author name are the only information a buyer sees, so it should be catchy and dynamic.

Subtitle (Optional)

This is a concise explanation, clarification, or amplification of the title. Keep this copy limited to one clear statement, not a long sentence. If you need to include more explanatory information, create a reading line or bullet points. Subtitles are usually used for nonfiction titles only; iUniverse will automatically add the words "A Novel" to the front cover of fiction titles.

Author name exactly as it should appear on the cover of your book. If applicable, enter a pseudonym, or pen name.

Co-author name, if applicable, exactly as it should appear on the cover of your book.

Please list the preferred author name, as well as the names of other contributors, exactly as you want it to appear on the cover and title page. If you want the role or title of the author and each contributor to appear on the cover and title page, list these as well. For example: William H. Doitright, PhD; or, Compiled by Will Doitright and Jim Smith; or William H. Doitright, PhD, with Illustrations by Ryan Hardy.

For front cover only: All of these items are *optional*; only include them if you feel the information enhances the title and subtitle or provides necessary marketing information. Be careful not to be repetitive.

Byline

The byline may include an author's credentials, affiliations (usually for nonfiction titles), or previous titles. On the front cover, this information will appear beneath or near the author's name. For example: Chief Clinical Psychologist, City University Hospital; or, Author of *Taking Charge*

Quote

An endorsement or an excerpt from a review would qualify as a quote for your front cover. Be sure to include the name and byline of the person who gave you the endorsement, because although you know the person's affiliations, readers may not. For example: "Never before has a book been so poignant and thought provoking. You must read this book!"—Thomas Smith, Author of *The Best You Can Be*

Reading Line (for nonfiction titles)
This gives the reader more detailed information about the subject and contents of the book. The reading line does not replace a subtitle, but appears in addition to the subtitle. For example: A Step-by-Step Guide to Balancing Your Life and Achieving Bliss

Bullet Points (for nonfiction titles)
Key words, phrases, or even short chapter titles from the book that detail the contents of the book in an easy-to-read format. The list should be parallel in construction. In other words, if you start the first item with a verb, subsequent items should also begin with a verb. In the list below, for example, if the first bulleted item stated, "Enjoy Your Job," the next bullet would not say, "Stress Reduction."

- Enjoy Your Job

- Relieve Stress

- Live a Healthy Lifestyle

- Exercise Regularly

- Improve Your Memory

Foreword
Add copy about the foreword to your front cover only if it was contributed by a prominent individual and may boost sales or public interest. For example: Foreword by Oprah Winfrey

Introduction
The criteria for adding front cover copy about the introduction is similar to that of the foreword copy: it should have an influential contributor to justify adding it.

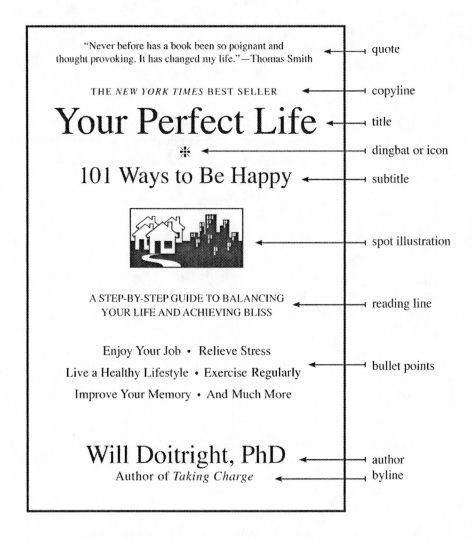

A **book description** of about three to four paragraphs describing the overall content of your book. This is intended for reference only and will not appear on the book.

This information is used to give people who work on your book an idea of what it's about, and it should include both a general statement about the book and some details about its content. This differs from the copy that will appear on the back cover of your book.

The exact name of the **copyright holder.**

If you wish to publish under a pseudonym, or pen name, use your pseudonym as the copyright holder so that your true identity does not appear in the copyright notice and remains anonymous.

Original year of copyright and the years of publication of any subsequent editions that appeared on the copyright page of the book. For new manuscripts, use the current year.

Note: iUniverse places the proper U.S. copyright notice in the front of each book but does not register the copyright on behalf of the author. It is the author's choice and responsibility to register the book with the U.S. Copyright Office.

Marketing and Book Cover Copy

The copy to be used on Web sites, in your Marketing Toolkit, and in the Printed Bookselling Materials. Be sure the copy is carefully proofread and enter it exactly as you would like it to appear, with no typos or errors. Please use plain text with no formatting and no html when writing your keynote and back cover copy. For example, do not use italics for the title of your book in the keynote or back cover copy.

The **keynote** or "elevator pitch," which should consist of one or two sentences (twenty-five word-count limit) that succinctly tell readers what the book is about and why they should buy it.

Imagine you have only ten seconds to tell someone about your book and convince him to buy it. What would you say? Be sure to avoid clichés. Also, it's often good to compare your book to a well-known author, title, or film to give a reader a point of reference. For example, "A veteran crime reporter delivers a hardboiled whodunit with *Die Hard*-type action, set in modern Chicago. The emerging Russian Mafia and diabolical political overtones both figure into this edgy, thrilling plot."

The **back cover copy,** a brief overview of the book, that entices the reader to browse and purchase the book. The ideal length is 150 to 200 words.

Think of this copy as a movie trailer or commercial—provide highlights, tease your audience, but don't give away the ending! This should not be a detailed, straightforward description of the book, but rather brief, pointed selling copy that is your promise to the reader: here's what my book is about, this is how it's unique, and this is why you should buy it.

In all marketing copy (keynote, back cover copy, and author bio), the following guidelines apply:

- Do not refer to the book as "the book." Use the book title, set in italics, in most cases.

- Avoid underlining words and using all caps.

- Do not refer to your audience as "the reader" or "readers." Write the copy in a manner that incites the reader to take action. For example, instead of "Readers will learn how to improve relationships with their pets," write, "Learn how to improve your relationships with your pets." Or, use a more direct statement, such as, "Learn how to improve your relationship with your dog, cat, or even parakeet." This approach lends a specific range and a casual tone to your book that can draw in the reader.

- Break up the book description into paragraphs. One long paragraph is very difficult to read. Bulleted lists help to tell the reader what's included in the book at a glance. If you include a bulleted list, make sure that you have a lead-in sentence followed by a colon, and that each item in the list has parallel construction. For example:
  - Create…
  - Learn…
  - Motivate…

  Not
  - Create…
  - Learning…
  - Motivation…

- Avoid clichés such as "a must-read" or "This book will change your life." The back cover copy is not a book review. It is a preview of the exciting world within.

- Keep the verb tense consistent throughout.

- If you need additional examples or ideas, look up books that compare and compete with your title and read the book descriptions on Barnes & Noble.com (www.bn.com). Better yet, go to your local bookstore and browse the section in which your book would ideally be shelved. Read the professionally created back cover copy of the bestselling titles in that genre; this will give you an idea of what readers will expect to see on your back cover.

- If you have advance praise (quotes, endorsements, or excerpts from advance reviews) you can include short excerpts with a credit line of the person who gave you the endorsement. Rather than just a name, provide the person's title or credentials as well; for example, for a book on speed walking you could list a quote from Cathy Smith, President, Northern California Speed Walking Association. It's best to use endorsements from people or periodicals that relate to your book in some way.

- The last paragraph of the copy should compel the reader to take action; it's the take-away promise of the book.

Hardcover flap and back cover copy, if chosen as an option during your submission.

Your hardcover edition will include a dust jacket with space for copy on the front and back flaps and on the back cover.

To conform to book-industry standard, we suggest the following:

Front Flap:

- Back cover copy from paperback edition.

Back Flap:

- Continuation of front cover copy, if necessary.

- Author photo (include credit if necessary); or, author photo may instead be placed on the back cover.

- Author bio from back cover of paperback edition.

Sample Back Cover Copy for Fiction

Cookin' for Love by Sharon Boorstin
Who Says Only Twentysomethings Can Have Fun, Romance, and Great Sex?

Married mother of three and Beverly Hills cookbook author Miriam Levy dreams about food. Her best friend, divorced Kate McGrath, dreams about "The One" who got away. When, after twenty-five years, Kate reconnects with her unforgettable first love on Google and he asks her to visit him halfway around the world (while his wife happens to be away), she begs Miriam to go with her. Reluctant but restless, Miriam agrees. Their overseas adventures awaken the women's spirits and teach them about passion, love, and life without regret.

Inspired by the author's own true story, *Cookin' for Love* is a funny and poignant tale about the comfort of friendship and the resilience of true love. With a hint of the forbidden, a dash of courage, and heaps of heart—along with twenty-five delectable recipes—this contemporary romp serves up all the ingredients for fine food, romance, and adventure.

"Exuberantly mixes the sweet things in life—love, friendship, family, and plenty of spice."
—*Kirkus Discoveries*

"Recipes sprinkled throughout the book add a delicious dimension to the tale."
—*Bon Appétit* magazine

"*Thelma & Louise* twenty years later. Entertaining and sweet."
—*The Austin Chronicle*

"A delicious confection that you'll want to devour to the last page."
—Iris Rainer Dart, Author of *Beaches* and *Some Kind of Miracle*

"A delicious story with all the trimmings of humor and womanspeak."
—Suzy Gershman, Author of *Born to Shop* and *C'est La Vie*

Sharon Boorstin has written for *More*, the *Los Angeles Times*, *L.A. Confidential*, *Jewish Woman* magazine, *Bon Appétit*, and more. She speaks to women's groups across America and has co-written screenplays for feature films and television. She was the restaurant critic for the *LA Examiner* and is also the author of *Let Us Eat Cake: Adventures in Food and Friendship*. Visit **www.cookinforlove.com**.

Sample Back Cover Copy for Nonfiction

Tilli's Story by Tilli Schultz and Lorna Collier
I think about what I want and what makes me happy,
But orderly and quietly to myself.
Because my thoughts tear down fortresses and walls,
My thoughts are free.
—German folk song, author unknown

The beautiful, safe, joyful places in young Tilli's imagination were her only refuge from the bombing that tore through the sky above her during World War II. Her thoughts were her only freedom from Hitler's Nazi tyranny, and they were her strength to survive after the war ended, when Russians invaded her tiny farming village in eastern Germany; forced her into months of hiding in a dark attic crawlspace; and took her innocence, her childhood, and nearly her life.

Tilli's dreams—of a time when she could think and act freely, and travel, work, write, worship, and live however she wished—were what fueled the sixteen-year-old to courageously and single-handedly escape the terror of Stalin's harsh Communist rule and create her own happy ending in a free America.

This true tale of sorrow and terror, hope and triumph, is Tilli's story—but it's also the story of the unthinkable suffering and untold bravery of countless innocent children who have lived through a war and its aftermath.

"A great piece of individual history from a woman who had some remarkable experiences…. Through this story, readers will come to appreciate more deeply ordinary citizens' experience of wartime and political upheaval, as well as the enormity of the decision to leave one's country and start a new life thousands of miles away."
—Lisa Seidlitz, PhD, Assistant Professor of German at Augustana College

Tilli Schulze was born in 1934 in eastern Germany. She escaped to West Germany in 1950 and immigrated to the United States in 1952, settling in northern Illinois. She and her husband Herbert have two grown children and three grandchildren. **Lorna Collier** is an award-winning writer who has worked as a daily newspaper reporter, magazine editor, and television news producer. She lives near Belvidere, Illinois, with her husband and two children.

Back Cover:

- Author photo, if not used on back flap (please specify the preferred size).

- Endorsements: Praise for a previous title or advance praise for current title with bylines.

- Fiction: A short passage from the beginning of the book that sets the tone or pulls the reader into the story.

- Nonfiction: A brief excerpt from the manuscript that shows the reader some key components or benefits of the book. Or, if the chapter titles of your book are particularly interesting or explanatory, put the table of contents on the back cover (with chapter and page numbers omitted). If you choose this last option, be sure to introduce the list with a phrase or sentence, such as, "Including the most complete, up-to-date information on:…" then list the chapter titles or an adapted version of them.

Key search words that will help people find your title through retail outlets. When you go to the library and search the card catalog by subject, or when you enter keywords on the Internet, you are using key search words. Key search words for a romance title might be *love, betrayal, romance, love affair, paramour, Paris*, and the type of romance (i.e., *gothic, regency, contemporary, historical*). There is no minimum number of words required, but the more words or phrases you provide that have a direct relation to the subject matter, the more opportunity people will have to find your book.

Target Audience

The **target age** group for your primary readers.

The target audience is a specific identification of the ideal group of customers who may buy a product. For a book, it's important to know who that audience is so that the tone and style of both the content of the book and its look is appropriate. You wouldn't write a casual, chatty book for a medical school textbook, but that would be the perfect style for a guide to dating. Everything about the book should be geared toward your target audience.

The **genre: fiction, nonfiction,** or **poetry.**

The **category** of your book chosen from a list of **general topics**.
The genre of fiction or nonfiction isn't enough to tell prospective buyers what your book is all about; you need a more focused category. If you've written a novel, is it a romance or a mystery? If it's nonfiction, is it a practical self-help book about parenting or dieting, or a narrative memoir or history? There are sections of the bookstore for practically everything. Think about where your book fits.

The category you choose for your book is important every step of the way, from the cover design, to the marketing copy, to the eventual pitch that you'll use in publicizing and promoting your book, and finally to your book's placement at both brick-and-mortar and online retailers.

STEP 4: UPLOAD YOUR FILE

A completed **manuscript**, which includes all the parts of the book in one document.

Traditional publishing houses provide certain *core services* to each and every book that goes out the door: copyediting, line editing, or content editing. A copyedit is a staple that every house relies upon, but many times, the work demands more attention. iUniverse offers an Editorial Evaluation as part of some of our publishing packages, which recommends the needed Editorial Services to give your book the professional polish it deserves. If you do not choose to use one of our professional service providers, please be certain that you submit a copyedited version of your manuscript, as this is what will appear in the final proofs of your book.

The Book Block

The inside of your book, which we call the book block, is divided into three main sections: the front matter, book block text, and back matter. It is important that your final submission to iUniverse include all three of these book parts in the correct order and format, combined in a single document. A checklist is included below. Those listed with an asterisk (*) are required; all else is optional.

Front Matter

❑ *Half Title Page

❑ Card or Series Title Page

❑ *Title Page

❑ *Copyright Page (iUniverse provides you with a standard copyright page that incorporates your individual information and ISBN.)

❑ Dedication

❑ Epigraph

❑ Table of Contents (Please do not include page numbers in your contents page; page numbers will be added by iUniverse during the formatting stage.)

❑ Acknowledgments

❑ List of Illustrations or Tables

❑ Foreword

❑ Preface

Book Block Text

❑ Introduction

❑ *Main Text (including parts, chapters, subtitles, text breaks, tables, and diagrams if applicable)

❑ Epilogue

❑ Afterword

❑ Conclusion

❑ About the Author(s)

Back Matter

❑ Appendix

❑ Notes

❑ Glossary

❑ Resources

❑ Bibliography or References

❑ Index

Parts of Your Book

Reference: University of Chicago Press. *The Chicago Manual of Style*, 15th ed. Chicago: University of Chicago Press, 2003.

Including all of the necessary parts of a book and putting them in the right order is the first step to making your book more credible and professional. The inside of your book, which iUniverse calls the **book block**, is divided into three main sections: the **front matter**, **book block text**, and **back matter**. Please make sure that the manuscript you submit to iUniverse includes all three sections combined into a single document and in the correct format. Below, see a detailed explanation and breakdown of each section.

Front Matter

Front matter introduces your book to your readers. The front-matter section, which appears before the main text, includes a few pages that include the book's title, the author's name, the copyright information, and perhaps even a preface or a foreword. Use the list of common front-matter pages below to identify those pages that are suitable for your book.

Half Title Page (required)

The half title page is the first page of your book and contains your title only. This page *does not* include a byline or subtitle.

Card or Series Title Page

Use the second page of your book to list any of your previously published books by title. It is customary to list the books chronologically from first to most recently published. Listing the title only is standard, but in nonfiction works, you may also list the subtitle if you feel it is essential. A common way to begin this page is: "Also by [author's name]…"

Title Page (required)

The title page shows your full book title and subtitle, your name, and any co-author or contributor. iUniverse will add its logo and locations at the bottom of the page.

Copyright Page

The copyright page contains the copyright notice, which consists of the year of publication and the name of the copyright owner. The copyright owner is usually the author but may be an organization or corporation. This page may also list the book's publishing history, permissions and acknowledgments, and disclaimers. *iUniverse provides you with a standard copyright page that incorporates your individual information and the ISBN (International Standard Book Number).*

Dedication

If you want to dedicate your book to someone special, be sure to include your tribute with your submitted manuscript. Dedications are usually short and directed at one person or family member. Keep it simple. You do not need to write "Dedicated to" or use headlines. Statements such as "For Mother" or "In Memory of My Father" are perfect.

Epigraph

If you have a simple quote or phrase that is significant to your book, you may want to consider adding it to the front matter of your manuscript as an epigraph. The source of the epigraph should be printed on the line under the quote or phrase. Please make sure you have permission to use your epigraph if it is beyond fair-use guidelines. If an extended credit line is required, put the credit line on the copyright page or in the acknowledgments section of your book, rather than under the epigraph.

(Table of) Contents

A table of contents is usually used only in nonfiction works that have parts and chapters. A contents page is less common in fiction works but may be used if your work includes unique chapter titles. A table of contents is never used if your chapters are numbered only (e.g., Chapter One, Chapter Two). If your book requires a contents page, please make sure it lists all the chapters or other divisions (such as poems or short stories) in your manuscript. Chapter listings must be worded *exactly* as they are in the book itself. *Please do not include page numbers in your contents page; page numbers will be added by iUniverse during the formatting stage.*

Acknowledgments

An acknowledgments page includes your notes of appreciation to people who provided you with support or help during the writing process or in your writing career in general. This section may also include any credits for illustrations or excerpts if not included on the copyright page. If the information is lengthy, some authors may choose to put the section in the Back Matter before or after the Bibliography.

List of Illustrations or Tables

If your book includes several key illustrations or tables that provide information or enhance the text in some way, consider creating a page that lists them. If this material is included simply for comic or visual relief, a page listing may not be necessary.

Foreword

The foreword contains a statement about the book and is usually written by someone other than the author who is an expert or is widely known in the field. A foreword lends authority to your book and may increase its potential for sales. If you plan to include a foreword, please arrange to have it written and included in your submitted manuscript. A foreword is most commonly found in nonfiction works.

Preface

The preface usually describes why you wrote the book, your research methods, and perhaps some acknowledgments if not included in a separate section. It may also establish your qualifications and expertise as an authority in the field in which you're writing. Again, a preface is far more common in nonfiction titles and should be used only if necessary in fiction works.

Book Block Text

The main text, or what we call the book block text, is the core of your manuscript. In the following outline of book block sections, find and use only the sections that apply to your manuscript. Make sure you combine each section into a single document, and submit them in the correct format to iUniverse.

Introduction

The introduction describes something about the main text that your reader should know before proceeding to read the rest of the book. Unlike a preface, which usually addresses the qualifications of the author, an introduction refers to the main body of the work itself. For example, if there are questions at the back of each chapter, here is where you might prepare the reader and give tips on how best to use them. Your introduction may also describe, in more detail than a preface, the research, methods, and overall concept of the book.

Main Text

Parts, chapters, headings and subheadings, text breaks, and tables and diagrams are good ways to organize and visually break up the monotony of your main text. The organization of your book should follow the logical progression of your ideas from the introduction to the conclusion. In nonfiction titles, the organization of your book and a brief outline of your content should be reflected on your contents page.

Here are a few ways to organize your main text:

- *Chapters and other divisions*—Most works of prose are divided into chapters. Chapter titles should be similar in tone, length, capitalization, and punctuation and be equally placed throughout your manuscript. If you include chapter titles, not just chapter numbers, they should be listed in the table of contents *exactly* as they are in the text. Books may also have divisions such as poems, short stories, or letters.

- *Parts*—When text can be logically divided into sections larger than chapters, the chapters may be grouped in parts. Each part is normally numbered and given a title, for example: Part One: The Basics. A part title should be added only if chapters can be appropriately grouped together under such a basic division title.

Epilogue

An epilogue is a brief concluding section, often addressed directly to the reader in a work of fiction. Most epilogues continue the story years later or update the reader on a certain character's whereabouts. Please do not use a chapter number for this section.

Afterword

The afterword is also a brief concluding section, often used in nonfiction works. It does not need a chapter number. If your book is about how to invest money wisely, for example, you may want to use the afterword to review the strategies outlined in your book and give some encouraging advice to help your reader move forward with the plan.

Conclusion

More extensive than an epilogue or afterword, a conclusion may or may not be numbered as the final chapter. The conclusion provides a summary of your ideas, concepts, and advice, leaving the reader with a clear understanding of the major concepts presented in the book and some guidelines on what to do with that information.

About the Author(s)

You may add a short biography at the end of your main text that summarizes (1) any expertise you have in the field in which you are writing, (2) any previous books that you have published, and (3) a brief summary of where you currently live, who you live with, and what type of work you do. If you'd like to include a photo of yourself, be sure to submit it to iUniverse with your final manuscript according to the required specifications.

Back Matter

Your book submission is not complete unless it includes the information that goes into the back of your book, or back matter. Does your book require notes? An index? Resources? To help you decide, we've provided the following descriptions for each of the common back-matter sections.

Appendix

An appendix includes any data that might help clarify the text for the reader but that would have disrupted the flow of the main text had it been included earlier. Some items included here might be a list of references, tables, reports, background research, and sources, if not extensive enough to be included in a separate section.

Notes

If your main text requires notes to amplify or document certain passages throughout the text, please arrange the notes by chapter in a notes section. Footnotes would more likely be included in the references section, described below.

Glossary

A glossary includes words arranged alphabetically and their definitions. Be sure to include one if you use terminology that is not generally known to the average reader or if you coin new words or phrases to explain your ideas.

Resources

Often readers want to buy products or join organizations in the field in which you've written. A list of organizations and associations, manufacturers and distributors, Web sites, and other sources is invaluable to your readers.

Bibliography or References

Both the bibliography and reference sections list the sources for works used in your book. Be sure to arrange the sources alphabetically by the author's last name. For samples and guidelines on proper layout, refer to the *Chicago Manual of Style,* 15th edition, or visit http://www.wisc.edu/writing/Handbook/DocChi_WC_book.html.

Index

The index is an alphabetically ordered list of words and terms used for referencing your text. Please keep in mind that a computer-generated keyword index, which lists a page number for a key term every time it occurs in your book, tends to be overly long and have no logical organization other than alphabetization. On the other hand, a professional indexer analyzes your entire book, anticipating line items your reader will most likely want to find, and listing them in an intuitive, accessible manner. For applicable titles, iUniverse offers for purchase the optional editorial service of a professional indexer who considers the focus, purpose, audience, and organization of your book to create an industry-standard, two-level index that is fully copyedited and proofread.

Art Files

The **art files** that will be uploaded for the cover of your book, including the exact credit lines.

Upload one of the following files:

- The exact design that should be used for the front cover.

- A file to be used as the illustration on the front cover in a design created by iUniverse.

- A file containing samples of artwork for reference ONLY; iUniverse will create a new illustration for the cover.

- A general idea for the cover, with no provided artwork, that iUniverse designers will use for reference ONLY.

The best way to guide our designers in creating your book cover is to provide a *general* idea of what you want. Authors who give minute details and specifications risk ending up with a cover that is a literal representation of one scene from the book and doesn't reflect current styles and trends in cover design. Great book covers are those that set a general tone or simply evoke what the book is about, are appropriate for the book's genre and category, and are eye-catching and will entice the reader to purchase.

iUniverse will make every effort to create a cover that satisfies both the author and the marketplace, however, we ask that you please be aware and considerate of time and budget restraints. We will only be able to match your requests in general, using the information you provide solely as a reference; we are unable to perform a photo shoot and some artwork may not be suitable for a professional cover. We are restricted to existing image availability but will do our best to meet the visual needs of your book and create a professional, appealing cover.

Note: If someone outside iUniverse has designed your cover, please include the name of the designer and any credit information in case it becomes the final design for your book. iUniverse cannot use images or designs without permission from the original artist.

Author photo for use on the back cover; note that photo placement may vary for each book. (Technical requirements for photographs are listed later.)

Make sure the author picture is done professionally. It doesn't need to be a studio shot with a prefabricated background or one taken at a mall photo shop, but a grainy snapshot is not suitable. You might get what you need from a friend or family member who has a digital camera with high resolution and who has some photographic abilities to capture the right composition and exposure for the shot.

Again, go to the bookstore and see what other author photos look like in books in your category. Are they informal photos taken in an author's home or yard? Or are they in a professional setting such as an office? What types of authors have their photos on the front cover? (Unless you're a celebrity or there is a very sound reason for your being on the front cover, we don't recommend that.) Although readers love to see what authors look like, if you're not happy with the image you portray, do without and concentrate on your author bio.

Interior graphic artwork (photographs and illustrations) that are to be included in your book.

Book cover illustrations (both front and back covers) and the author photo are included in the base price of your submission. Interior book illustrations require an extra charge of $100 for 1–25 graphics and $200 for 26–50. If you have more than fifty interior illustrations, please contact Submission Inquiries for more information.

Be sure to read and comply with the specifications for photographs and artwork that follow in the next section. Submit the best-quality photographs possible since muddy shots and old, faded photographs are difficult to print.

Find and Upload Your Files

A completed **manuscript** in Microsoft Word with at least 10,000 words or 48 pages (104 pages for a hardcover edition). Your manuscript must be submitted as a single file.

Cover design photo and illustration files that must be in the TIFF (.tif) image file format, in CMYK, with a 300-dpi resolution, and it must match the dimension of the final trim size, plus a 1/8" bleed on the top, right, and bottom sides. It is not advisable to use borders on your cover. *Not applicable to Fast Track.*

An **author photo** in the TIFF (.tif) image file format, in CMYK, with a 300- or 600-dpi resolution and a 2" × 2" printed size. Optional for Select, Premier, and Premier Plus. *Not applicable to Fast Track.*

A separate file for each **photo** or **illustration** that will be placed within the **interior** of the book. Each file should be in the TIFF (.tif) image file format, in grayscale, with a 300-dpi resolution, as well as embedded in your manuscript exactly where you want it to appear. *Not applicable to Fast Track.*

STEP 5: COMPLETE YOUR SUBMISSION

Royalty Allocation and Payment Information

The **Social Security Number** or **Tax Identification Number** for each royalty participant listed in Step 1. This is required for U.S. residents only.

iUniverse is committed to keeping all financial information you provide strictly confidential.

The **percentage of royalties** each individual or entity should receive.

Direct deposit option, if the participant wishes to receive royalty payments via direct deposit (ACH Credit). Pertinent direct deposit information will be gathered after the submission process is complete. This option is available for use with U.S. banks only.

Additional Publishing Services

iUniverse offers a variety of optional services. Although some of these services are included in the economical publishing packages we offer, if you did not choose one of the all-inclusive packages, you may always elect to add the following a la carte services; find prices on our Web site.

OCR Service

This option is available for authors who do not have their files in the proper electronic format and need text scanning and conversion of tables, photographs, or other graphic images.

Cover Copy Polish

The text on the cover of your book can make or break a prospective reader's buying decision. If you select this option, a marketing professional will assist you in rewriting the hardcover flap copy (if applicable), back cover copy, author bio, keynote, and key search words. This feature is included in the Premier Plus package.

Editorial Evaluation

An Editorial Evaluation is a manuscript checkup that will provide you with constructive feedback from independent publishing pros. In addition, if your book receives a positive Editorial Evaluation, you'll be eligible for many of our special programs and marketing services and our full range of editorial services, including those listed below (see **Editorial Services** on our Web site). This option is included in the Premier Plus and Premier packages.

Line Editing

Select this option, and an editor will check your manuscript line-by-line and correct errors in spelling, grammar, punctuation, and word choice; the editor will also make suggestions for better sentence structure and impose industry-standard style. If you receive an Editorial Evaluation, you will be referred to the exact level of editing needed.

Proofreading

As any publishing professional knows, the production process is not 100 percent foolproof. At traditional publishers, all manuscripts are proofread at least once during the final stage before a book is printed. Select this option and your manuscript will get a careful character-by-character proofread.
Prerequisite: *iUniverse Line Edit or referred iUniverse Editorial Service.*

Indexing

Publishing professionals, such as reviewers, know the importance of a quality index. To maximize the usability of a nonfiction title, an index is generally recommended. Our indexers will provide you with an industry-standard, two-level topical index. This is not a computer-generated index, which is generally not very useful, but one that is compiled specifically for your book's subject matter and target audience.

Hardcover

If you select this option, your manuscript will also be produced as a 6" × 9" hardcover book.

Marketing Success Workbook

An effective marketing plan is perhaps the most important element of any successful self-published book. Select this option and you'll receive the Marketing Success Workbook—a step-by-step guide that will show you how to develop an innovative and comprehensive marketing plan designed specifically for your book.

Kirkus Discoveries Book Review

If you choose this option, your book will be reviewed by Kirkus Discoveries. Kirkus is well-known and trusted within the publishing industry for promoting and building awareness of a variety of titles.

Printed Bookselling Materials—Quantities of 100–400

Choose this option and receive professionally designed, full-color postcards, bookmarks, and business cards featuring your book.

Google Book Search

If you choose, iUniverse will enter your book into the Google Book Search Partner Program, a specialized search on Google.com.

Press Materials

Using information you provide, our publicity staff creates a basic publicity package for your book, including a unique selling point or hook, a cover-letter template, and a press release.

Clipping Service

When you subscribe to our clipping service, iUniverse will monitor more than 18,000 publications nationwide for your name and the title of your book.

Your Publishing Agreement

The **publishing agreement** associated with the publishing package you have selected. In order to continue with the next phase of publication, you will need to accept the agreement by checking the box located below it, and then typing in your name and the date of acceptance.

Billing Address

Your correct **billing address**.

Payment Information

Order review. Confirmation of other editorial and marketing services. The **promotional code** that applies special terms, if any.

Throughout the year, iUniverse offers authors various special discounts and programs; please check our Web site for the current month's special offering and enter your code as requested.

Credit card information, including type, number, and expiration date to complete your **payment**.

Confirmation/Receipt

Receipt page that can be reviewed and printed. You will also receive an e-mail containing your confirmation information.

myUniverse link, provided to log in to your account.

This link is set up just for your use and is password protected. Once you are logged in, you will be prompted to complete any additional information that might be necessary for the specific publishing program you have selected. Your myUniverse link will be a primary source of information for you throughout the publishing process—from submissions information to eventual royalties and sales.

Publishing Checklist for Manuscript Submission

Following is a list of information and materials you'll be asked to provide during your online submission. Compiling this in advance will make the submission process easier and faster. If you have questions, please contact 1-800-AUTHORS x504. An iUniverse publishing professional will be happy to help you every step of the way.

Note: You can download the Publishing Checklist for Manuscript Submission from iUniverse.com/getpublished.

Authors and Other Royalty Participants

❑ **Contact information** such as address, phone number, and e-mail address that will be used to correspond with you throughout the publication process.

❑ The **name of each individual or entity** that will receive a portion of the royalties generated from the sale of your published book.

❑ The **type of royalty participant**, such as author, co-author, agent, corporation, or organization.

❑ The **primary contact** for all publishing correspondence.

Author Biography

❑ An **author biography** to be included in your book, placed on the iUniverse Web site, and provided to book wholesalers and retailers.

Information about Your Book

❑ The **title**

❑ The **subtitle** (optional)

❑ The **author name** exactly as it should appear on the cover of your book. If applicable, enter a pseudonym or pen name.

❑   **A co-author name**, if applicable, exactly as it should appear on the cover of your book.

❑   **Additional copy for front cover** should be added only if appropriate.

❑   **A book description** consisting of approximately three to four paragraphs describing the overall content of your book. This is intended for reference only and will not appear on the book.

❑   The exact name of the **copyright holder**. If you wish to publish under a pseudonym or pen name, list your pseudonym as the copyright holder so that your true identity does not appear in the copyright notice and remains anonymous.

❑   **Original year of copyright** and the years of publication of any subsequent editions that appeared on the copyright page of the book. For new manuscripts, use the current year.

Note: iUniverse places the proper U.S. copyright notice in the front of each book but does not register the copyright on behalf of the author. It is the author's choice and responsibility to register the book with the U.S. Copyright Office.

Marketing Copy

❑   The **keynote** or "elevator pitch" that consists of one or two sentences (25 word-count limit), which succinctly tell readers what the book is about and why they should buy it.

❑   The **back cover copy**, a brief overview of the book that entices the reader to browse and purchase the book. The ideal length should be 150 to 200 words.

❑   **Key search words** that will help people find your title through retail outlets.

Target Market

❑   The **target age group** for your primary readers.

❑ The **genre**: fiction, nonfiction, or poetry.

❑ The **category** of your book, chosen from a list of general topics.

Photo and Illustration Files

❑ The **cover photo and illustration files** that will be uploaded for the cover of your book, including the exact credit lines. The uploaded file will either be the exact design that should be used for the front cover; a file to be used as the illustration on the front cover in a design created by iUniverse; a file containing samples of artwork for reference ONLY and iUniverse will create a new illustration for the cover; or a general idea for the cover with no provided artwork that iUniverse designers will use for reference ONLY.

Note: If someone outside of iUniverse has designed your cover, please be certain to include the name of the designer and any credit information, in case it becomes the final design for your book.

Caution: iUniverse cannot use images without permission from the original artist.

❑ An **author photo** for use on the back cover; note that photo placement may vary for each book.

❑ The number of **interior graphics** (photographs and illustrations) that are to be included in your book.

Note: Book cover illustrations (for both the front and back covers) and the author photo are included in the base price of your submission. If you only plan to submit cover illustrations and the author photo, then choose "None." Interior book illustrations require an extra charge of $100 for 1–25 graphics and $200 for 26–50. If you have more than 50 interior illustrations, please contact Submission Inquiries for more information.

Find and Upload Your Files

❑ A completed **manuscript** in Microsoft Word or Word Perfect format with at least 10,000 words or 48 pages (104 pages for a hardcover edition). Must be submitted as a single file.

❑ **Cover design** photo and illustration files, which must be in the TIFF (.tif) file format, in CMYK, with a 300-dpi resolution and matching the dimension of the final trim size plus a 1/8" bleed on the top, right, and bottom sides. It is not advisable to use borders on your cover. *Not applicable to Fast Track.*

❑ The **author photo** in the TIFF (.tif) file format, in CMYK, with a 300- to 600-dpi resolution and a 2" × 2" printed size. Optional for Select, Premier, and Premier Plus. *Not applicable to Fast Track.*

❑ A separate file for **each photo or illustration** that will be placed within the **interior** of the book. Each file should be in the TIFF (.tif) file format, in grayscale, with a 300-dpi resolution, and be placed in your manuscript exactly where you want it to appear. *Not applicable to Fast Track.*

Royalty Allocation Information

❑ The **Social Security Number** or **Tax Identification Number** for each royalty participant listed in Step 1: Authors and Other Royalty Participants. Required for U.S. residents only.

❑ The **percentage of royalties** each individual or entity should receive.

❑ The **direct deposit** option, if the participant wishes to receive royalty payments via direct deposit (ACH Credit). Pertinent direct deposit information will be gathered after the submission is complete. This option is available for use with U.S. banks only.

Additional Publishing Services

❑ Optional **editorial services.**

❑ Optional **book marketing services.**

❑ Optional **hardcover edition.**

❑ Optional **OCR.**

Your Publishing Agreement

❏ The **publishing contract** associated with the publishing package you have selected. In order to continue with the next phase of publication, you will need to accept the contract by checking the box located below it, and typing in your name and the date of acceptance. Please print a copy of this contract for your records.

Billing Address

❏ Your correct **billing address.**

Payment Information

❏ An **order review.** Confirmation of other editorial and marketing services purchased by clicking on the Additional Services link.

❏ The **promotional code** that applies special terms, if any, activated by clicking the Validate button.

❏ **Credit card information** including type, number, and expiration date to complete your payment.

Confirmation/Receipt

❏ A **receipt page** that can be reviewed and printed. You will also receive an e-mail containing your confirmation information.

❏ A **myUniverse link,** provided to log in to your account. Once logged in, you will be prompted to complete any additional information necessary for the publishing program you have selected.

Appendix C

AFTER PUBLICATION

Your relationship with iUniverse doesn't end once your book has been produced. Our staff is here to help you track your book sales, offer marketing support, and assist you with book orders.

ORDERING BOOKS

Book Orders

To purchase copies of your own books with your author discount (as defined in your publishing agreement), please contact the iUniverse customer service department:

Toll-free in the United States: 1-800-AUTHORS x501
International callers: 402-323-7800 x501
E-mail: book.orders@iuniverse.com

Once we have received your order, we will e-mail, fax, or call you to provide an order confirmation with your Sales Order Number. If you do not receive a confirmation message from us, then for some reason, we did not receive your order. Once your order has been printed, assembled, and boxed, you will receive a second confirmation e-mail that includes your UPS tracking number (if you selected UPS delivery). You can then track your order at

UPS.com. To check the status of a non-UPS shipment, please contact customer service. Book orders cannot be cancelled and are nonrefundable, except in the event of poor print quality. Please report quality or quantity issues to the book orders department within three business days of your receipt of the order.

Book Discounts for Author Events

iUniverse offers a special discount to authors who have arranged events such as book signings. To qualify for this discount, the event for which the books are purchased must be listed in the iUniverse Author Event Calendar located on our Web site: iUniverse.com. This calendar can be accessed directly from your myUniverse account. Submit your event by clicking on the Add Event link. Your event will receive approval within two business days, at which point you may order books at a discount. All books must be drop-shipped directly to the retail outlet or public venue hosting the event.

For Retailers: A retail book signing special discount of 40 percent off the list price will apply to purchases of twenty or more copies made by retail outlets— defined as vendors purchasing books for resale directly to the consumer—for a public author event at a recognized venue.

For Authors: An author book signing special discount of 45 percent off the list price will apply to purchases of twenty or more copies made by an author for a public author event at a recognized venue. Note that author purchases are royalty exclusive.

Volume Discount Pricing for Authors

If you are interested in purchasing multiple copies of your book to send to the media for publicity outreach or for special sales purposes, iUniverse offers the following volume discounts:

Discount Pricing for Authors	
Book Quantity	Discount Off List Price
1–5	30%
6–19	35%
20–99	40%
100–249	45%
250–499	50%
500–999	55%
1,000–1,999	60%
2,000+	65%

Paperback

Retail Discounts

It is standard practice in the publishing industry for different types of retailers to receive discounts on book purchases. By purchasing a book at a discount and then reselling it at the full list price, the retailer earns money. Different categories of retailers receive different discount rates.

At iUniverse, the discount given to retailers corresponds to the royalty rate selected by an author. Most iUniverse contracts pay a 20 percent royalty to authors, and the corresponding retailer discount is shown in the center column in the table below. Authors who select our Premier or Premier Plus packages have the option to select a 10 percent royalty rate in exchange for deeper discounts to retailers, as shown in the column to the right. Increasing the discount makes your book more attractive to booksellers and easier for them to stock your book. Booksellers highly value deeper discounts on the books they purchase.

	Royalty Choices	
	20%	10%
Discounts		
Institutions	20%	25%
Retail	25%	30%
Retail DC	30%	35%
Wholesale	36%	50%

Royalties
Royalty Calculations

Royalties are based on the payments we actually receive from the sales of printed or electronic (eBook) copies of your book, not including shipping and handling charges, or sales and use taxes. Unlike some publishing-service providers, we do not deduct production or printing costs when calculating net receipts. We offer discounts to retail and wholesale customers, so the royalty amount you receive depends upon which type of customer bought your book and any discount they received. (See *Retail Discounts* above.)

Author book purchases are royalty exclusive. You will earn royalties on all books not purchased by yourself or by a co-author.

Royalty Payments

Author royalties are paid according to calendar quarters:

Quarter	Month	Royalty Paid
First Quarter	January–March	May 30
Second Quarter	April–June	August 29
Third Quarter	July–September	November 29
Fourth Quarter	October–December	March 1

iUniverse will process your royalty payment, in accordance with our publishing agreements, sixty days after the end of each quarter. For example, January through March is the first quarter. We will post your royalty statement and send your payment by May 30. It takes a few weeks for purchases to show up on your royalty statements, so don't be alarmed if your current statement doesn't show all of the purchases that you believe took place during a given quarter.

Direct Deposit Program

If you sign up for our convenient Direct Deposit program, all the royalties you have earned will be paid directly into your checking account. If you have not yet signed up for our Direct Deposit program, and the royalty amount you have earned is less than $25, it will be carried forward and added to the royalties you earn in the next quarter.

Refer-a-Friend Program

Our Refer-a-Friend program pays you $100 when you refer a new author to iUniverse. To refer a friend, log in to your myUniverse account on our Web site and click on the Refer-a-Friend button. Simply fill out the online form with the names and e-mail addresses of up to four authors who could benefit from our services. You'll receive $100 for each referred author who publishes a book with us within the six months following your referral. The Refer-a-Friend program is open only to existing iUniverse authors. In order to be paid for the referral

- You must post the referred author's name and e-mail address prior to the referred author's submission.

- The name and e-mail address of the referred author must exactly match the name and e-mail address used for the referred author's book submission.

For more information about the Refer-a-Friend program, log in to your myUniverse account and click on the Refer-a-Friend button, or speak with one of our representatives at 1-800-AUTHORS x504.

Appendix D

THE iUNIVERSE
EDITORIAL GUIDE

You've accomplished something most people only dream of—you've written a book. Because you've worked hard to get to this point, you deserve to have the same editorial resources and information available to you as traditionally published authors have. That's why we've created the iUniverse Editorial Guide.

The Editorial Guide is by no means a substitute for an Editorial Evaluation or an Editorial Service; however, it can act as a checklist to help you (1) include the right type of content in each section of your book and place each part in the appropriate order, (2) format paragraphs and characters correctly, and (3) understand and interpret the comments and changes suggested by iUniverse editorial evaluators and editors. In short, the Editorial Guide can help you create a book that is more compelling, effective, and competitive.

The Editorial Guide is not an exhaustive list of guidelines. If you encounter issues or questions not covered here, we recommend that you consult the following main sources used by our professional evaluators and editors—the same industry-standard resources on which most major traditional book publishers rely:

- *The Chicago Manual of Style*, 15th ed. Chicago: University of Chicago Press, 2003.

- *Merriam-Webster's Collegiate Dictionary*, 11th ed. Springfield, MA: Merriam-Webster, 2003.

CONTENTS

Now that you've written the main parts of your book, how should you piece them all together? You want to include a section that thanks your loved ones for supporting you while you were writing, but is that included on the acknowledgments page or a dedication page, and does it go before or after the table of contents? And how do you include a list of the sources you used? The first part of this guide will describe the appropriate content and subject matter to include in each section of your book and will help you put all the parts in the right order.

How do you indent a recipe or a poem? What is an em dash? And how do you type ellipses? (We'll give you a clue: it's not by pressing the period key three times.) Part II of the Editorial Guide will help you to know when and how to apply typefaces (such as boldface or italics), punctuation marks, and indents to format your manuscript in a way that is attractive, effective, and easy to read.

Your line editor suggested changing a sentence from passive to active voice, but how do you do that? And when exactly do you use a semicolon instead of a comma? How should you write specific numbers such as dates or percentages? Part III answers in plain English our authors' most frequently asked questions about punctuation, grammar, spelling, and other editorial issues.

Part I
Parts of Your Book

Including all of the necessary parts of a book and putting them in the right order is the first step to making your book credible and professional. The inside of your book, which we call the **book block**, is divided into three main sections: the **front matter**, **book block text**, and **back matter**. Please make sure that the manuscript you submit to iUniverse includes all three sections combined into a single document and in the correct format. See a detailed explanation and breakdown of each section below, followed by a checklist to help you ensure your book includes all the necessary parts.

Front Matter

Front matter introduces your book to your readers. The front-matter section, which appears before the main text, comprises a few pages that include the book's title, the author's name, the copyright information, and perhaps even a preface or a foreword. Use the list of common front-matter pages below to identify those pages that are suitable for your book.

Half Title Page (required: author must provide)
The half title page is the first page of your book and contains your title only. This page *does not* include a byline or subtitle.

Card or Series Title Page
Use the second page of your book to list any of your previously published books by title. It is customary to list the books chronologically from first to most recently published. Listing the title only is standard, but in nonfiction works, you may also list the subtitle if you feel it is essential. A common way to begin this page is "Also by [author's name]…"

Title Page (required: author must provide)
The title page shows your full book title and subtitle, your name, and any cowriter or translator. iUniverse will add its logo and locations at the bottom of the page.

Copyright Page

The copyright page contains the copyright notice, which consists of the year of publication and the name of the copyright owner. The copyright owner is usually the author but may be an organization or corporation. This page may also list the book's publishing history, permissions and acknowledgments, and disclaimers.

Note: iUniverse provides you with a standard copyright page that incorporates your individual information and the ISBN (International Standard Book Number).

Dedication

If you want to dedicate your book to someone special, be sure to include your tribute in the manuscript you submit. Dedications are usually short and directed at one person or family member. Keep it simple. You do not need to write, "Dedicated to" or use headlines. Dedications such as "For Mother" or "In Memory of My Father" are perfect.

Epigraph

If you have a simple quote or phrase that is significant to your book, you may want to consider adding it to the front matter of your manuscript as an epigraph. The source of the epigraph should be printed on the line under the quote or phrase. Please make sure you have permission to use your epigraph if it is beyond fair-use guidelines. (Stanford University has a set of fair-use guidelines available at http://fairuse.stanford. edu/Copyright_and_Fair_Use_Overview/ chapter9/index.html. Also, see a sample letter for obtaining permissions at the end of this style guide.) If an extended credit line is required, put the credit line on the copyright page or in the acknowledgments section of your book, rather than under the epigraph.

(Table of) Contents

A table of contents is usually used only in nonfiction works that have parts and chapters. A contents page is less common in fiction works but may be used if your work includes unique chapter titles. A table of contents is never used if your chapters are numbered only (e.g., Chapter One, Chapter Two). If your book requires a contents page, please make sure it lists all the chapters or other divisions (such as poems or short stories) in your manuscript. Chapter listings must be worded *exactly* as they are in the book itself.

Please do not include page numbers in your contents page; iUniverse will add page numbers during the formatting stage.

Acknowledgments

An acknowledgments page includes your notes of appreciation to people who provided you with support or help during the writing process or in your writing career in general. This section may also include any credits for illustrations or excerpts if not included on the copyright page. If the information is lengthy, you may choose to put the section in the back matter before or after the bibliography.

List of Illustrations or Tables

If your book includes several key illustrations or tables that provide information or enhance the text in some way, consider creating a page that lists them. If this material is included simply for comic relief or as a visual aid, a page listing may not be necessary. Just as with the table of contents, you won't need to list the page numbers.

Foreword

The foreword contains a statement about the book and is usually written by someone other than the author who is an expert or is widely known in the field of the book's topic. A foreword lends authority to your book and may increase its potential for sales. If you plan to include a foreword, please arrange to have it written and included in your submitted manuscript. A foreword is most commonly found in nonfiction works.

Preface

The preface usually describes why you wrote the book, your research methods, and perhaps some acknowledgments if they have not been included in a separate section. It may also establish your qualifications and expertise as an authority in the field in which you're writing. Again, a preface is far more common in nonfiction titles and should be used only if necessary in fiction works.

Book Block Text

The main text, or what we call the book block text, is the core of your manuscript. In the following outline of book block sections, find and use only the sections that apply to your manuscript. Make sure you combine each section into a single document, and submit it in the correct format to iUniverse.

Introduction

The introduction describes something about the main text that your reader should know before proceeding to read the book. Unlike a preface, which usually addresses the qualifications of the author, an introduction refers to the main body of the work itself. For example, if there are questions at the conclusion of each chapter, here is where you might prepare the reader and give tips on how best to use them. The introduction may also describe, in more detail than a preface, the research, methods, and overall concept of the book.

Main Text

Parts, chapters, subtitles, text breaks, and tables and diagrams are good ways to organize and visually break up the monotony of your main text. The organization of your book should follow the logical progression of your ideas from the introduction to the conclusion. In nonfiction titles, the contents page should reflect the organization of your book and a brief outline of its content.

Here are a few ways to organize your main text: (1) *Chapters and other divisions*—Most works of prose are divided into chapters. Chapter titles should be similar in tone, length, capitalization, and punctuation and be equally placed throughout your manuscript. If you include chapter titles, not just chapter numbers, they should be listed in the table of contents *exactly* as they are in the text. Books may also have divisions such as poems, short stories, or letters. (2) *Parts*—When text can be logically divided into sections larger than chapters, the chapters may be grouped in parts. Each part is normally numbered and given a title, for example, Part One: The Basics. A part title should be added only if chapters can be appropriately grouped together under such a basic division.

Epilogue

An epilogue is a brief concluding section, often addressed directly to the reader in a work of fiction. Most epilogues continue the story years later or update the reader on a certain character's whereabouts. Please do not use a chapter number for this section.

Afterword

The afterword is also a brief concluding section, often used in nonfiction works. It does not need a chapter number. If your book instructs readers how to invest money wisely, for example, you may want to use the afterword to review the strategies outlined in your book and give some encouraging advice to help your readers move forward with the plan.

Conclusion

More extensive than an epilogue or afterword, a conclusion may or may not be numbered as the final chapter. The conclusion provides a summary of your ideas, concepts, and advice, leaving the reader with a clear understanding of the major concepts presented in the book and some guidelines on what to do with that information.

About the Author(s)

You may add a short biography at the end of your main text that summarizes (1) any expertise you have in the field in which you are writing, (2) any previous books that you have published, and (3) a brief summary of where you currently live, who you live with, and what type of work you do. If you'd like to include a photo of yourself, be sure to submit it to iUniverse with your final manuscript according to the required specifications.

Back Matter

Your book submission is not complete unless it includes the information that goes into the back of your book, or back matter. Does your book require notes? An index? A resource list? To help you decide, we've provided the following descriptions for each of the common back-matter sections.

Appendix

An appendix includes any data that might help clarify the text for the reader but that would have disrupted the flow of the main text had it been included earlier. Some items included here might be a list of references, tables, reports, background research, and sources, if not extensive enough to be included in a separate section.

Notes

If your main text requires notes to amplify or document certain passages throughout the text, please arrange the notes by chapter in a notes section. Footnotes would more likely be included in the references section, described below.

Glossary

A glossary comprises alphabetically arranged words and their definitions. Be sure to include one if you use terminology that is not generally known to the average reader or if you coin new words or phrases to explain your ideas.

Resources

Often, readers want to buy products or join organizations in the field in which you've written. A list of organizations and associations, manufacturers and distributors, Web sites, and other sources is invaluable to your readers.

Bibliography or References

Both the bibliography and reference sections list the sources for works used in your book. Be sure to arrange the sources alphabetically by the author's last name. For samples and guidelines on proper layout, refer to the *Chicago Manual of Style,* 15th edition, or consult the notes provided by the University of Wisconsin–Madison on the Internet: http://www.wisc.edu/writing/Handbook/DocChi_WC_book.html.

Index

The index is an alphabetically ordered list of words and terms used for referencing your text. Please keep in mind that the computer-generated keyword index that lists a page number for a key term every time it occurs in your book tends to be overly long and has no logical organization other than alphabetization. On the other hand, a professional indexer analyzes your entire book, anticipates subject items your reader will most likely want to find, and lists them in an intuitive, accessible manner. For applicable titles, iUniverse offers for purchase the optional editorial service of a professional indexer who considers the focus, purpose, audience, and organization of your book to create an industry-standard, two-level index that is fully copyedited and proofread.

Parts of Your Book Checklist

Using the preceding descriptions of each section, circle the elements below that apply to your book. Then put a checkmark next to each of your circled elements after you complete it. Sections listed with an asterisk (*) are required for all titles.

Front Matter
- ❑ *Half Title Page
- ❑ Card or Series Title Page
- ❑ *Title Page
- ❑ *Copyright Page (iUniverse provides you with a standard copyright page that incorporates your book-specific information and ISBN.)
- ❑ Dedication
- ❑ Epigraph
- ❑ Table of Contents (Please do not include page numbers in your contents page; page numbers will be added by iUniverse during the formatting stage.)
- ❑ Acknowledgments
- ❑ List of Illustrations or Tables
- ❑ Foreword
- ❑ Preface

Book Block Text
- ❑ Introduction
- ❑ *Main Text (including parts, chapters, subtitles, text breaks, tables, and diagrams if applicable)
- ❑ Epilogue
- ❑ Afterword
- ❑ Conclusion
- ❑ About the Author(s)

Back Matter
- ❑ Appendix
- ❑ Notes
- ❑ Glossary
- ❑ Resources
- ❑ Bibliography or References
- ❑ Index

Note: You may download this checklist at iUniverse.com/getpublished

PART II
Layout and Formatting

Formatting refers to the way you enter paragraph and line breaks, indents, spaces, typefaces, and punctuation marks. By observing a few basic text-formatting rules, you can help us transform the pages of your manuscript into a final book that looks attractive and professional.

Paragraph Breaks and Indents

To view all of the spaces, hard returns, and tabbed areas in your manuscript as symbols, select the **Show All** character (¶) in your Microsoft Word toolbar. If you can't find this character in your toolbar, hold down the *Ctrl* and *Shift* keys and press the 8/* for the same results.

Paragraphs
Paragraphs are separated with one paragraph mark (¶). This is also referred to as a hard return, usually accessed by pressing Enter on your keyboard. Lines within a paragraph must continue (or wrap) at the margin; lines should not be broken with paragraph marks or manual line breaks.

First-Line Indents
The first paragraph in each chapter or part should *not* be indented. However, the first line of all other paragraphs should be indented with one tab.

Indents
To indent a block of text, such as a passage from a referenced source, highlight the section of text you want indented, select **Format** in the toolbar, and then choose the **Paragraph** option in most word processors. Indent the paragraph on the left and right each by one-half of an inch (0.5").

Single-Line Indents
To indent individual lines, such as in a poem or a recipe, use two tabs.

Dashes, Hyphens, and Ellipses

Dashes, ellipses, and other special characters are found under the **Insert** menu of your word processing program, under **Symbol/Special Characters.** (See the punctuation section of Part III to learn more about when to use these marks.)

Do not use double dashes (--) to express a pause in a thought or duration of time. Instead, use the longest dash, called an **em dash** (—), or an ellipsis (…) to separate thoughts or clauses within a sentence. To type an em dash, hold the Ctrl and the Alt key and type a hyphen, or hold down the Alt key while typing 0151. See instructions below for typing an ellipsis.

Use en dashes (–) (the longer dash) to separate periods of time or numbers. To type an en dash, hold the Ctrl key and type a hyphen, or hold down the Alt key while typing 0150.

Use hyphens (-) (on your keyboard) to separate two words that are usually linked with a hyphen.

Ellipses Hold Ctrl + Alt + the period key.

Italics

By going to the font settings in your word processing software (under **Format** in the toolbar), or by holding down Ctrl + I, you may apply italic type for the following reasons:

- Titles of books, magazine articles, movies, plays, television shows, and other titles of major works
- Words with emphasis (use sparingly)
- Foreign words and phrases

Formatting to Avoid

ALL CAPS

Do not use all caps for emphasis, for titles, or for contents pages. WORDS TYPED IN ALL CAPS ARE DIFFICULT TO READ. Use italics instead.

Underlining

Underlined text usually looks old-fashioned. Use italics to express emphasis or to indicate key terms instead, but even then, use sparingly.

Centered Text

Limit the use of centered text. It looks overly formal and can be hard to read.

Manual Hyphenation

Do not manually hyphenate words that break at the end of a line. Both your word-processing software and our book-design software will automatically hyphenate words when necessary.

Quotation Marks

Straight quotation marks are not acceptable substitutions for traditional quotation marks. When straight quotes appear, please exchange them with "curly" quotes (called smart quotes). Microsoft Word may be set to display smart quotes by default through the AutoCorrect menu. Please consult the Help documentation of your word processing software for more information. Or correct individual straight quotation marks as follows: for a smart open quote, press Alt + 0147. For a smart closed quote, press Alt + 0148.

PART III
Editorial Style

What Is Editorial Style?

Editorial style is commonly confused with writing style. While writing style may refer to a writer's unique voice or application of language, editorial style refers to a set of guidelines that editors use to help make your words as consistent and effective as possible. A good book editor will be sensitive to maintaining a balance between your unique writing style—your voice—and editorial style. Studies have shown that consistent editorial style not only lends credibility to your work, but also makes it easier to read and understand.

What Editorial Style Does iUniverse Follow?

iUniverse evaluators and editors follow the same industry-standard style guidelines as most major traditional book publishers. Below, we've listed the style reference and dictionary used by our evaluators and editors. Editors and evaluators may allow exceptions to the standard guidelines depending on the book's context or on an author's specific request.

Editorial References

- *The Chicago Manual of Style,* 15th ed. Chicago: University of Chicago Press, 2003.

- *Merriam-Webster's Collegiate Dictionary,* 11th ed. Springfield, MA: Merriam-Webster, 2003.

Here is a synopsis of some of the editorial guidelines followed by iUniverse editors and evaluators:

Dates and Numbers

These rules apply to the format and style of numbers as they appear in most manuscripts

- July 3, 1974 (Use a comma before and after the year in running text.)

- 1977–99 (Truncate numbers in year ranges.)
- Spell out whole numbers one through one hundred.
- Spell out round numbers greater than one hundred (e.g., two hundred, fifty thousand, etc.).
- Spell out any number beginning a sentence.
- Centuries should be spelled out and lowercased (e.g., the twenty-first century).
- Hyphenate the "tens" and "ones" places in combination numbers (e.g., the one hundred and twenty-fifth anniversary).
- Use hyphens to separate the digits in a telephone number (e.g., 1-800-288-4677).
- Always use numerals with percentages. In general copy, spell out *percent* (e.g., 89 percent). In scientific or technical contexts, use % without a space preceding the symbol (e.g., 89%).
- When using numerals to express monetary amounts, use the symbols $ or ¢ (e.g., $45, 53¢). When monetary amounts are spelled out, also spell out *dollars* or *cents* (e.g., forty-five dollars, fifty-three cents).

Capitalization

- Do not capitalize an entire word or phrase for emphasis; use italics instead.
- Use small caps without periods for AM and PM (e.g., The train left at 6:00 PM.).
- Do not capitalize offices or titles unless used as part of a proper noun (e.g., Abraham Lincoln was the president of the United States. *but* Students often study the life of President Abraham Lincoln.).
- Capitalize personifications (e.g., Mother Nature).
- Bulleted or numbered list items should begin with a capital letter.
- Do not capitalize *him, his,* or other pronouns referring to deities, such as Jesus. (Most Bible translations follow this style.)

Punctuation

Commas

Use a comma for the following reasons:

- Between two independent clauses joined by a conjunction. An independent clause is a clause that can stand alone as a sentence (e.g., I took my shoes off, and I walked on the grass. *but* I took my shoes off and walked on the grass. Because "walked on the grass" does not have a separate subject ["I"] in the second example, it is not an independent clause. Therefore, no comma is used.).

- To separate elements in a series. iUniverse prefers its authors use a comma before the conjunction that precedes the final element in the series, called the series or serial comma (e.g., I learned about stars, comets, and planets.).

- Before and after the name of a state that is preceded by the city in the middle of a sentence (e.g., One thing and one thing only put South Elgin, Illinois, on the map.).

- With introductory phrases (e.g., Finally, they reached their destination.), in direct address (e.g., Thank you, Mom.), and after yes and no (e.g., Yes, that's what he said.), especially if a slight pause is intended.

- To separate two adjectives that precede and modify a noun (e.g., He drove the old, rusted car. *but* He drove the light green car.).

Hyphens, En Dashes, and Em Dashes

The hyphen (-), the en dash (–), and the em dash (—) all have different purposes and should be used in different situations. All three marks run flush to the text on both sides (with no space on either side).

Hyphens

- Use hyphens in compound words and to separate characters (in phone numbers, for example).

Ex.

That is some heavy-duty machinery!

He started working a part-time job.

I placed a toll-free call to a 1-800 number.

- Hyphenate adverb + adjective compounds before, but not after, the nouns they modify unless they appear hyphenated in Merriam-Webster (e.g., much-loved woman *but* the woman was much loved).

- Compounds with *most* and *least* and adjectives ending in -ly are not hyphenated (e.g., the beautifully decorated house).

- Hyphenated adjectival compounds that appear in Merriam-Webster's should be spelled with a hyphen when they follow a noun (e.g., Your point is well-taken.).

En dashes and em dashes
- The en dash is generally used with number ranges to signify *up to and including, to,* or *through.* Do not use an en dash if the word *from* or the word *between* precedes the first element.

Ex.

You'll find the Lord's Prayer in Matthew 6:7–13.

The measure passed with a vote of 154–17.

The war years, 1939–45, were difficult.

OR

The war lasted **from** 1939 **to** 1945.

I lived in Vermont **between** 1984 **and** 1986.

- To enter an en dash in Microsoft Word, hold the Ctrl key and press the minus key on the number keypad, or hold down the Alt key while typing 0150.

- The em dash (commonly called a dash) is used to set off a statement within a sentence. It is also used to indicate sudden breaks in dialogue. Do not use a space before or after the em dash.

  > Ex.
  >
  > Eric—having just discovered the letter—ran down the street after his car. She read works by the beat authors—Kerouac, Ginsberg, and Burroughs—and it showed in her writing.
  > "I think you should consid—" was all I heard before the phone went dead.

  To enter an em dash in Microsoft Word, hold the Ctrl and the Alt key and press the minus key on the number keypad, or hold down the Alt key while typing 0151.

Colons and Semicolons

- A colon is often used to introduce an element or series of elements. It can also be used between two independent clauses (similar to the semicolon) to emphasize sequence.

  > Ex.
  >
  > There are four states of matter: liquid, solid, gas, and plasma.
  > I didn't feel threatened by them: after all, I had seen them fight before.

- A semicolon is often used to separate two independent clauses not joined by a conjunction.

  > Ex.
  >
  > We reached a fork in the road; two of us went left, and the other three went right.

- "When a colon is used within a sentence…the first word following the colon is lowercased unless it is a proper name. When a colon introduces two or more sentences…or when it introduces a speech in dialogue or an extract…the first word following it is capitalized" (*CMS* 6.64).

Ellipses

- Use ellipses to indicate broken, stuttered, or interrupted dialogue and incomplete sentences.

- If the omitted material appears immediately after a complete sentence, use a period followed by Microsoft's Word's ellipsis character (created by holding the Ctrl + Alt + period keys).

- When using the "four-dot method" (in which the ellipsis appears after a period) put a space after the ellipses, but not before (....). When only three dots are used, put a space before and after the ellipsis (...).

Grammar
Only use nor *with* neither.

Write parallel sentences

When a sentence contains two or more ideas that are parallel, try to construct each idea in the same way grammatically.

> Ex.
>
> **Unparallel**: The manager was responsible for **writing** orders, **counting** inventory, and **to organize** the stock room.
>
> **Parallel**: The manager was responsible for **writing** orders, **counting** inventory, and **organizing** the stock room.

> OR
>
> **Unparallel**: It would be easier **to take** the train than **changing** your flight.
>
> **Parallel**: It would be easier **to take** the train than **to change** your flight.

Avoid passive sentences

Use passive sentences sparingly, if at all. Because passive sentences usually only show who or what is *receiving* the action, they leave the reader wondering about who or what in the sentence is *performing* the action. Another tip-off that a sentence is passive is that it usually contains some form of the verb *to be* (e.g., is, are, was, were, had been).

Ex.

Passive: The meeting **was** held last night. (*Who* held the meeting? The meeting is *receiving* the action.)

Active: The **student council held** the meeting last night. (The student council held the meeting and is *giving* the action.)

OR

Passive: To accomplish this, the following had **to be** considered… (*Who* had to consider the following?)

Active: To accomplish this, **she** had to **consider** the following…

Make nouns and pronouns agree

Ex.

Incorrect: **A student** must work hard if **they** want to be at the top of **their** class.

Correct: **A student** must work hard if **she** wants to be at the top of **her** class.

Correct: **Students** must work hard if **they** want to be at the top of **their** class.

Check your modifiers

The best way to check your modifiers is to find sentences that begin with the action rather than the actor. Once you figure out what the action is in the first portion of your sentence, just make sure that you clearly identify the actor in the second part of the sentence. If the actor is not identified, then you've probably got a *dangling modifier*.

Ex.

Incorrect: Driving to New England in the early fall, **the trees** had begun to turn beautiful colors. (*The trees* were not driving.)

Correct: Driving to New England in the fall, **we** saw that the trees had begun to turn beautiful colors. (*We* were driving.)

Abbreviations

*   U.S. (United States)—use this abbreviation only as an adjective. As a noun, spell out "United States."

*   For all other abbreviations, use periods with lowercased abbreviations, but use no period between the letters of an abbreviation in full or small caps (e.g., a.k.a., OPEC, NRA).

*   Use *i.e.* and *e.g.* only between parentheses, set in a normal type (not italic or boldface), and followed by a comma.

Word Choice and Consistency

*   Capitalize brand names (e.g., Popsicle, Kleenex, Kool-Aid).

*   Use American English (e.g., criticize *not* criticise) unless the context, setting, or audience dictates otherwise.

*   When *Merriam-Webster* lists multiple spellings of a single word, use the topmost spelling (e.g., judgment, *not* judgement).

Commonly Misspelled and Mis-capitalized Words
Acknowledgments (no *e* after the *g*)
Foreword (not Forward)
Internet (always with a capital *I*)
Web site (two separate words, always with a capital *W*)
e-mail (with a hyphen after the *e*)

In-Text References
Do not use in-text references that refer the reader to a particular page or page number (e.g., on the previous page *or* on page 52). When your book is converted from an 8.5" × 11" page, the formatting and page numbers change, making all such references invalid. If you do make in-text references, either make them relative (e.g., later in this chapter, in chapter 5, in the following paragraph) or be sure to correct these after your book is formatted.

Citation, References, and Bibliographies

Authors have two main choices for dealing with sources:

1. Use author-date parenthetical citations within the text, paired with a bibliography.

2. Use endnotes and a bibliography.

Author-Date System

When you use something specific from a source, such as a quote or a paraphrase, one option is to use a parenthetical text citation in author-date style. (If you use this method, you will need a bibliography.) For example,

> **A dog can improve your life by giving you unconditional love, developing responsibility in your children, providing you with security against intruders, and perhaps even lowering your blood pressure (Wyant 1999, 29).**

Endnotes/Bibliography

Another option is to create a footnote. Here is an example of how a small numeral is placed within the text to reference a footnote:

> **Many people have found that caring for these loving companions has actually resulted in lower blood pressure.** [1]

The reader can then look to the corresponding footnote to find information on the book you quoted. In a book, endnotes appear at the end of a chapter or, more commonly (because easier to locate), at the back of the book. If you put your endnotes at the back of the book, strongly consider including a bibliography to expand on any publication information that does not appear in the endnotes. Endnotes are preferred over footnotes for books that appeal to scholarly and general audiences. Here is an example of a footnote that would be used in conjunction with a full bibliography:

> 1. Wyant, *The Dog Lover's Guide to Life,* 29.

The corresponding bibliographic entry would give more information:

Wyant, Wendy. *The Dog Lover's Guide to Life: How Your Dog Can Make You a Better Person.* New York: Star Spirit Press, 1999.

Bibliography Style
iUniverse follows the style below for referencing books and periodicals in bibliographies.

Referencing books
Lastname, Firstname. *Book Title.* City, State of Publication: Publisher's Name, Year.

Referencing periodicals
Lastname, Firstname. Year. Title of journal article. *Journal Name* Vol: Page–Range.

Permissions
If you've borrowed material from other copyrighted sources, you may find yourself wondering whether you need to seek written permission to use another author's words or thoughts. While you must cite the source for every quotation or paraphrase you decide to use, some borrowed material requires further permission from the copyright owner before it can be used in your book.

If you're still unsure whether you need to seek permission, refer to chapter 4, "Rights and Permissions," in the *Chicago Manual of Style.* You can also look to the Web site of the National Copyright Office at http://www.copyright.gov/fls/fl102.html.

Once you've determined what permissions are necessary, you'll need to send a formal request to the copyright holder. Our Sample Permissions Letter on the next page provides a helpful template for preparing your requests.

Sample Permissions Letter

[Date]   Material Covered by This Request:
                          Chapter: Manuscript Page:
[Author Name]   Figure/Table Number:
[Address]

Dear Permissions Editor:

I am working with iUniverse, Inc. to publish a [**genre of book**] titled [**book title**] by [**author(s)**] in [**year of publication**]. As the author, I would like to secure the permissions for the material specified above.

The text will be a [**type of book: hardbound, paperback, etc.**] with approximately [**number of pages**] pages. Because iUniverse utilizes print-on-demand technology, there will be no first-print run. The average print-on-demand title sells less than five hundred copies. The probable cost will be [**estimated price**]. I am requesting world rights for the material described below and will be grateful for your permission to use it in this edition of the book as well as in subsequent editions.

I will give full credit to the author and publisher, either as a footnote or as a reference within the text, or both.

I have provided a release form below. Please sign to grant permission and fax or mail this form to my attention at [**fax number or address**]. Your prompt attention is appreciated.

Sincerely,

Permission is granted for the use of the material as stipulated above:

Name: _____ Date: _____

GLOSSARY

Acknowledgments. An author's notes of appreciation to people who provided support or help during the writing process or during the author's writing career in general. This section usually appears at the front of the book and may also include any credits for illustrations or excerpts if not included on the copyright page. If the information is lengthy, some authors choose to put the section in the back of the book.

Acquisitions Board. Group of people working for a publisher who decide what books to accept for publication; staff members may represent editorial, marketing, and sales departments, and include upper management.

Advance. Money paid to an author for royalties anticipated from the sale of the book before the royalties are actually earned. The total sum is usually divided into payments upon the publisher's countersigning of the contract, upon delivery and acceptance of a finished manuscript, and upon publication. The higher the advance, the more the total payment is spread out.

Advance Print Run. Quantity of a book printed before the book's official release date.

Appendix. Part of book that follows a chapter (end-of-chapter appendix) or that, more commonly, follows all the chapters (end-of-book appendix). An appendix provides easy accessibility to reference material and contains supplemental material, such as tables or source material, that does not conveniently fit into a chapter.

Attachment. Computer file that travels with an e-mail message.

Back Matter (End Matter). Counterpart of front matter. Any material, such as appendixes, notes, references, glossary, or index, that follows the chapters of a book.

Back-of-the-Room Sales. Sales of a book that happen in conjunction with the author's spoken presentation or participation in a conference, in which the author is generally represented as an expert on the subject matter being covered. Such sales are often made at a table at the back of the auditorium or in the hallway.

Bleed. An illustration, graphic, or other element that extends outside the normal trim area to the edge of a page. If extended to the outer edge of a page, such elements have ink that is visible on the edge of the page in the bound book.

Blog. An online journal (a shortened form of *Web log*).

Blogging. Writing and maintaining a blog.

Book Block. PDF files that comprise all book content except the cover. *See also* **PDF (Portable Document File).**

Book Club. Commercial enterprise that offers periodical (often monthly) selections of books to its paid membership. Special book club editions of books may have a different binding or size from standard-issue books from the same publisher. A book club may also be a group of people who gather to discuss a chosen title; Oprah's televised book club is an example of a more informal reading group in which the readers do not necessarily meet in one place. Typically, however, readers' book clubs consist of people meeting at a common time and place to discuss a particular title.

Book Doctor. An experienced editor who provides a deep structural edit for a book manuscript. A book doctor actually revises the manuscript; *compare* **Developmental Editor.** Also, the procedure of improving and reorganizing the structure, content, and order of a book manuscript.

Brick-and-Mortar Retailer. Retailer who sells products in a physical store. The term is often used to show the contrast between *e-tailers* (online sellers) and those who sell their products at a walk-in location.

Category. The subject matter of a book or area of a retail store such as mystery, self-help, biography, or other area. The category of the book often appears on the back cover of paperback titles. *Compare* **Genre.**

CMYK. Refers to the four colors of ink used in printing most books and photographs. The initials stand for cyan (C), magenta (M), yellow (Y), and black (K). Printing is done in layers, one color at a time. RGB colors, or those used on computer screens, do not correspond exactly to CMYK specifications; therefore, the image on a computer screen appears different from the way it appears in print.

Content Editor. Editor who addresses the content (subject matter) of a book in addition to its form (sentence structure). A content editor often recommends somewhat substantive corrections to a manuscript, such as those affecting presentation, veracity, relevance, continuity, and consistency of ideas.

Co-op Advertising. Advertising whose cost is shared among different contributors such as publishers, authors, and retailers. Such advertising is especially advantageous to smaller companies and authors with limited budgets. Such ads are also called *cooperative advertising*. In some *co-op advertising*, a publisher or manufacturer offers incentives or discounts to retailers who promote particular books or products.

Copyeditor. An editor who cleans up minor errors in a book, such as those in grammar, punctuation, spelling, usage, and style.

Copyright (Copyright Page, Copyright Notice). Ownership of intellectual property such as printed matter, protected by law. The right to copy, repurpose, or publish content of the copyrighted medium.

Co-venture. A publishing arrangement or partnership in which costs and responsibilities are shared by more than one company or publisher; also called a joint venture.

Cover Design. The layout of the front cover of a book including all cover copy (title, subtitle, bylines, and copylines) and any art if included.

Credit Line. Line of text that gives credit to the owner of the copyright of the material it refers to.

Design (Book and Cover). Layout, selection of font and font size, and typesetting of a book. *See* **Cover Design.**

Developmental Editor. Editor who gives a detailed assessment and suggestions about the overall organization of a book manuscript rather than making direct changes to grammar, spelling, content, sentence structure, and typographical errors. A developmental editor may also suggest reorganizing chapters and blocks of text, and may address tone, voice, extensive addition or deletion of material, complexity of material, transitions among paragraphs and sections of the book, and pacing. A developmental editor gives advice about the book's structure but does not make actual revisions. *Compare* **Book Doctor.**

Discount (Short Discount, Deep Discount, Industry-Standard Discount). Reduced book price offered to retailers, consumers, and authors: short discount (a smaller than average discount); deep discount (a large discount); industry-standard discount (one that corresponds to what most companies in a particular industry grant to retailers); author discount (given to authors who purchase their own books in bulk quantities). Many retailers also offer discounts to consumers for best sellers or to members of frequent-buyer programs.

Disintermediation. Business arrangement in which there is no middleman in a transaction.

Distributor. Company, group, or individual who sells and ships products to retailers instead of to consumers. *Compare* **Wholesaler.**

Domain Name. Registered Web address of a particular party. Registration often requires a small fee that prevents other parties from registering the same name.

Download. To move file(s) from a server, from a network, or from the Internet to a computer. To move file(s) from a computer to a diskette, CD, or memory stick. *Down* implies moving to a smaller device. *Compare* **Upload.**

DPI (Dots per Inch). The graphic resolution (grain) of a graphic file on a computer monitor, or the potential printing density of a computer printer. *See* **Resolution.**

eBook. Electronic file format in which books may be published. Although dedicated devices may be used to read eBooks, these electronic books can be read on other platforms such as personal computers.

Economy of Scale. Principle that production of larger volumes of something tends to reduce unit cost, because fixed costs are distributed across a greater quantity of a product. Savings in per-unit cost is achieved with mass production.

Editorial Rx Referral. Referral to an editorial specialist, if needed, by a professional evaluator. The referral informs both the author and an editor about the editorial needs of a given title.

Endorsement (Blurb, Testimonial). Promotional statement by someone recommending a book, often found on the cover or near the front of the book.

Footnotes (Endnotes). Reference citations and other supplementary information that appears at the bottom of a book page. A footnote is denoted in the text by a number, set in superscript type; *endnotes* take the same form as footnotes but appear at the end of the chapter or book, rather than at the end of the page.

Formatting. Process by which a design team lays out a manuscript to create book pages and applies text effect to characters to make them appear bold, italic, sheared, or otherwise.

Genre. Broad category or subject of a book, such as fiction, nonfiction, and poetry. *Compare* **Category.**

Ghostwriter. Professional writer contracted by an author or publisher to write or cowrite a book. A ghostwriter's work often goes uncredited upon publication.

Grayscale. Images composed of varying shades of black and white. Grayscale images may originally have been represented in color.

Halftone. A method of representing the colors of an image with dots of varying sizes. If the dots are small enough, the colors of the image appear continuous. Halftones are created to prepare photographic images for reproduction among various print media.

Hardcover Book. Book that has cloth or paper glued to board material, forming a durable cover and spine.

Index. Alphabetical list of words at the end of a book that guides a reader to the specific pages on which subjects appear in the main body of the text.

Interior Graphics. Pictures, diagrams, figures, photographs, and other graphical items that appear within the contents of a book.

International Standard Book Number (ISBN). Unique thirteen-digit number (although prior to 2007, number may contain ten or thirteen digits) that identifies a version of a book.

JPEG (Joint Photographic Experts Group). A digital format used for the compression and storage of high-quality photos and other graphic images.

Key Word. A word or phrase typed into a search engine or database that can lead a person to information on a particular subject or product in an online search.

Line Editor. Editor who performs work on a book manuscript that is heavier than copyediting, considering voice, tone, and phrasing.

Literary Agent. Experienced professional who can place a title with a publisher and advocate for an author in negotiations and transactions with the publisher.

Makeready Stage. Point in the printing process when the final version of the manuscript is prepared for printing.

Manuscript. Complete draft of a book (often an electronic file created with word processing software) prepared by the author. Also refers to both textual and graphic elements of the book. Editors and authors make preproduction book alterations to the manuscript. The finalized manuscript is used to produce the interior of a book.

Marketing. Promotional and advertising efforts to sell books.

Mass-Market Paperback. Small, inexpensive version of a book often sold in non-bookstore outlets, such as grocery stores and airports. *Compare* **Trade Paperback.**

myUniverse. Personal, secure Internet account provided to an iUniverse author, which permits the author to check the status of the book's progress throughout the publication cycle and facilitates the transmittal of book materials.

Networking. Expanding one's social network or sphere of influence by initiating mutually advantageous relationships.

Newswire Distribution. Service provided by an organization of journalists to circulate news reports among media outlets.

Niche. Term referring to a specialized target market characterized by a particular interest, topic, or subject.

Nonexclusive Contract. Legal agreement in which the publisher does not exercise exclusive rights over the materials in the author's book and in which the author retains control over how long the publisher may keep the book in distribution.

OCR (Optical Character Recognition). Computer program that can scan a hard copy of a manuscript and translate the words and images into a digital file.

Offset Printing. Common printing technology that applies one layer of ink at a time to paper using a roller.

Off-the-Book-Page Attention. Coverage of a book outside the context of a book review; for instance, mention of a book in a local news or features section of a newspaper.

Online Bookseller (Online Retailer). Bookstore on the Web that sells books and other publications to customers at retail or discounted prices.

Online Marketing. Advertising, selling, or dispensing products through the Internet.

Out of Print. Description for a book that is no longer in a traditional publisher's book inventory (and for which there are no republication plans).

Out of Stock. Status of a book for which no inventory is available; usually a temporary status that occurs while books are reprinted.

Page Proofs. A version of the manuscript after it has been typeset displaying all text and graphics as they will appear in the final book. Page proofs also contain running heads (the chapter or book title found at top of pages) and page numbers.

Pay-per-Click Advertising. Arrangement between a Web site host and an advertiser in which the advertiser pays the host a set amount when a visitor to the site clicks on that ad.

PDF (Portable Document Format). The electronic file format often sent to and used by a printer to produce final copies of a book. PDF files are used in conjunction with Adobe Systems programs.

Permission. Agreement from a copyright holder that permits the reproduction or publication of copyrighted material.

Plant Costs. Set-up costs incurred by a traditional printer for the initial printing of a given title. Total cost may include preparation of negatives and plates, and press preparation. Plant costs are fixed, but they are proportionately and increasingly offset as the number of copies printed increases.

Plot. Flow or succession of action in fiction.

Podcast. Audio broadcast available on the Web to the public for downloading to a personal computer or a digital audio player. Despite its name, a podcast may be played through a variety of digital audio software and hardware; its use is not limited to the iPod brand products developed by Apple.

Point of View. A narrative technique that captures a particular character or person's perspective in fiction pieces; for example, the use of first-person (told from the perspective of a character directly involved in the story, using the pronoun *I*), third-person (portraying the feelings, thoughts, and ideas of a character in the story, using pronouns such as *he* or *she*), or omniscient (told by an uninvolved third person who knows everything about the characters and can share all things with the reader).

Print-on-Demand (POD). Publishing model in which books are printed in single or small quantities only as orders are placed.

Print-Ready. Final PDF files of a book that are ready to go to the printer. *See also* **PDF (Portable Document File).**

Proofreading. Final editorial polish of a typeset manuscript to check for small remaining errors such as those in formatting, grammar, punctuation, and spelling. Proofreading can be performed only on manuscripts that have previously received the appropriate editorial service.

Publication Date. Official date when a book is to be released to the public.

Publicist. Trained professional who promotes a book among the three media outlets—print, radio, and television—and may arrange public appearances or events, such as readings and book signings.

Publicity Tour. Public circuit an author makes to publicize a book soon after the publication date. Typical places and appearances include book signings at bookstores or book shows, talk show appearances on radio and television, and interviews with the press. Publicity tours are usually booked only for celebrity or best-selling authors.

Remainder. Books that are returned to the publisher after not having sold, often offered for later sale at a discounted price.

Resolution. The number of pixels, or dots, per inch that make up a piece of art or a photograph; generally, the higher the resolution, the clearer the image will be when printed.

Return on Investment (ROI). Amount of profit made after investment costs and other costs have been recouped.

Returns. Overstock of books returned to and refunded by the publisher in full after failing to sell through retail outlets.

Review. Professional book reviewer's published opinion of a particular book in a periodical or online.

Royalty. A percentage of a book's sales revenue paid to the author.

Running Head. Text at the top of a standard book page that usually contains book, chapter, or section title information. A recto (right-hand page) running head usually contains different content from that on the verso (left-hand page).

Self-Publishing. Book-publishing model in which an author assumes full control of the publishing process as well as the total financial risk of publishing a book. Often, self-published authors bear the responsibility and cost of the book's distribution and marketing. Self-publishing circumvents the need for an author to contract with a publishing house to ensure publication of a book. *See also* **Subsidy Publishing; Supported Self-Publishing.**

Sell Sheet. Concise, one-page document that provides details about a book and how to order it.

Shelf Life. Time an unsold book remains on the shelf of a retail store before being replaced by a newly published title.

Slush Pile. Unsolicited manuscripts received by a publishing house or literary agency.

Small Press. Smaller publishing house that releases books often intended for specialized audiences.

SMART. Mnemonic acronym that summarizes the five essential qualities of effective goals. *SMART* reminds authors to set priorities that are $\underline{S}$pecific, $\underline{M}$anageable, $\underline{A}$ttainable, $\underline{R}$ealistic, and $\underline{T}$ied to time.

Spine Width. Width of the part of the book that connects the front and back covers and is visible when books are put onto a bookshelf.

Subsidiary Rights. Rights acquired by a publisher for licensing to other companies, such as rights that allow the book to be translated into foreign languages or presented in audio format, and rights that allow the reuse of a book's content.

Subsidy Publishing. A *subsidy publisher* shares publishing costs with the author and typically helps the author market the book through retailers. The author bears at least some of the cost of copyediting, typesetting, proofreading, indexing, and printing. Some subsidy publishers require an author to purchase a large number of copies to cover the costs of its initial printing. *Compare* **Self-Publishing; Supported Self-Publishing.**

Supported Self-Publishing. Method of self-publishing espoused by iUniverse, through which an author has access to many of the services found in a traditional publishing house (such as editorial and marketing services) provided through an upfront cost or available à la carte. The author also maintains a majority of the control in supported self-publishing. *Compare* **Self-Publishing; Subsidy Publishing.**

Table of Contents. This section, usually titled simply *Contents*, appears in the book's front matter and lists each chapter as it appears in the book and its opening page number.

Target Audience. Specific group of people to whom a book, series, or genre is likely to be sold. Book marketing and publicity tend to be directed toward a target audience.

Teleseminar. Seminar, lecture, or discussion available through a telephone or Internet-based conference call. *Compare* **Webinar; Webcast.**

Termination Clause. Section in a contractual agreement that specifies particular behavior, actions, events, or situations that would result in nullification of the contract.

TIFF (Tagged Image File Format). Compressed-file format preferable for higher-quality graphic images.

Title. A descriptive heading, such as the name of a book or chapter. Also a published work; for example, "approximately 195,000 titles were published in 2004."

Trade Paperback. A book bound with a paper or heavy stock cover, usually with a larger trim size than a mass-market paperback. *Compare* **Mass-Market Paperback.**

Trade (Mainstream, Traditional, Commercial) Publishing. Traditional model of publishing in which an author must find a literary agent or publisher willing to review and publish the manuscript. Trade publishers do not produce academic, professional, or educational titles but rather books for the general public.

Trim Size. Physical dimensions of a book page after the book is bound and trimmed.

Typesetting. Formatting a book electronically with the desired layout, font, and appearance.

University Press. Publishing house owned and operated by a university. Such presses typically issue academic or literary material, often including the works of professors at the institution.

Unsolicited Manuscript. Manuscript sent to a publisher or agent who did not request it.

Upload. To move an electronic file from a computer to a server, a network, or the Internet. Or to move the file from a diskette, CD, or memory stick to a computer. *Up* implies moving to a larger device. *Compare* **Download.**

Vanity Press (Vanity Publisher). Publisher that prints books financed entirely by their authors for the sole purpose of providing author satisfaction. The author sometimes retains the copyright. Books are not distributed through retail channels.

Virtual Book Tour (VBT). Advertising strategy centered on publicizing a book via the Internet, including book giveaways and ads on Web sites that the target audience frequents.

Webcast. A one-way Internet broadcast of a live or previously recorded seminar or interview. Webcasts are generally not interactive or designed for digital downloading. *Compare* **Podcast.**

Webinar. Scheduled seminar broadcast accessed through the Web. Like normal seminars, Webinars are interactive.

Webring. Collection of associated Web sites with similar themes that may be accessed through hypertext links.

Wholesaler. Company, group, or individual who purchases high volumes of books from a publisher at deep discounts and resells them to retailers at mid-level discount.

Word of Mouth. Free advertising for a book after its release, achieved when satisfied readers recommend the book to others. Ideally, consumers create a buzz that in turn creates publicity.

INDEX

Contact iUniverse

1-800-AUTHORS (288-4677)

or 1-402-323-7800

iUniverse, Inc.

2021 Pine Lake Road

Lincoln, Nebraska 68512

www.iUniverse.com

978-0-595-39573-6
0-595-39573-2

Printed in the United States
65263LVS00006B/104